discover libraries
This book should be returned on or before the due date.

To renew or order library books please telephone 01522 782010
or visit https://lincolnshirespydus.co.uk
You will require a Personal Identification Number
Ask any member of staff for this.
The above does not apply to Reader's Group Collection Stock.

EC. 199 (LIBS): RS/L5/19

*In memory of my father, John Valentine
- prolific writer and producer of pantomimes for the
Birstall Methodist Church Men's Pantomime. Over a period of
over forty years he wrote, produced and directed all of the
classic pantomimes, raising tens of thousands of pounds for the
Church and other charities. They are still produced to this day
every year to full capacity audiences.*

*My grateful thanks to all at the East Bridgford Drama Group
for the inspiration to write this and for their support.*

*A special mention to Dave Darby of East Bridgford
and Radcliffe Drama Societies for his helpful and
knowledgeable suggestions.*

But most of all, thanks to Jackie.

All Washed Up!

A Two-Act Play -
part mayhem, part pantomime

David Valentine

J. Garnet Miller

Copyright © by David Valentine in 2013
The right of David Valentine to be identified as the author of this work has been asserted by him in accordance with the Copyright, Designs and Patents Act 1988.

First published by J. Garnet Miller
(A division of Cressrelles Publishing Company Limited)
10 Station Road Industrial Estate, Colwall, Malvern WR13 6RN
Telephone/Fax: (01684) 540154

Possession of this book confers no right of licence to produce or give a reading of this play, publicly or privately, for charity or for gain, without first obtaining permission from the publisher or our agents. A fee is payable on each and every performance. A performance is any presentation or preview to which an audience, of any size, is admitted. Charitable institutions and non-profit-making organisations are NOT exempt from paying royalties, whether or not admission is charged. Requests for information about fees and for a licence to perform this play should be made to the publishers or our agents:
DALRO: *PO BOX 31627, 2017 Braamfontein, South Africa*
Drama League of Ireland: *Mill Theatre, Dundrum Town Centre, Dundrum, Dublin 16*
Origin Theatrical: *PO BOX Q1235, QVB Post Office, Sydney, NSW 1230, Australia*
Play Bureau: *PO BOX 9013, St Clair, Dunedin 9047, New Zealand*

Whenever this play is produced, the name of the author must appear on all publicity for the play. The programme must also contain the following notice: "By arrangement with Cressrelles Publishing Company Ltd."

Copying or reproducing, without permission, all or any part of this book, in any form, is infringement of copyright. Failure to observe any of the above stipulations, or any other provisions of the copyright laws, is breach of copyright. All persons who are party to the infringement are liable to both civil and criminal proceedings.

A CIP record for this book is available from the British Library.
ISBN: 978-0-85343-693-5
Printed in the UK by Cressrelles Publishing Company Ltd.

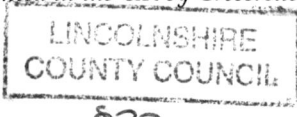

Characters

Alex - Stagehand, young(ish), jeans and t-shirt
Jeffrey - Stage Manager, older, jeans and t-shirt
Poppy - Prompter, up to middle-aged
Bea - Props/costumes, young(ish), a bit dizzy, dresses outrageously
Lawrence - Director, up to middle-aged
Jasmine - Leading Lady (and Dame), older
Rupert - Leading Man (and Baron), older
Old Woman/Fairy - Any age, ckeaning lady
Voice of *Amanda*
Sound and Lighting Effects Team - occasionally vocal, can be the real team or a dummy team.

First performed in November 2012, by the East Bridgford Drama Group, with the following cast:

Alex - Christian King; *Jeffrey* - Len Jackson
Poppy - Naomi Cope; *Bea* - Karen Peckover
Lawrence - Chris Wynne; *Jasmine* - Jean Starbuck
Rupert - Geoff Soar; *Old Woman/Fairy* - Pam Dawson
Sound Box - Jeff Casterton

Set Design - Geoff Soar; Graphics - Jon Shepherd
Lighting - Duncan Garment; Sound - Jon Shepherd
Directed by David Valentine

Scene

The play opens on the unfinished set of a pantomime - *Jack and the Beanstalk*. There is a pathetic-looking beanstalk on set and also a part-built cottage*. The cottage is on the edge of a village, with a road leading off to the market, via the dark wood.

* Note - the cottage flats need to be very light-weight. The back and sides can be part-constructed, but the front needs to be lying around on set. It is going to be gradually constructed, but will collapse in the final scene!

Act I, Scene One

*During this scene, the **Sound and Lighting Team** continually make adjustments - lights come on and off intermittently, as well as random sound effects occurring. The remaining wall(s) of the cottage lie on their side ready to be put together.*
Jeffrey *is eating a bag of chips out of newspaper.* ***Alex*** *is absent-mindedly wiring a motor which appears to control the beanstalk.*
Poppy**, **Bea** and **Lawrence *are looking at costumes in a box.*
Lawrence *is clearly harassed and keeps ticking items off on his clipboard, whilst struggling with his manbag.*

After a few moments, a central spot comes on, the rest of the stage lights dim. ***Alex*** *moves into the spot, the others freeze -* ***Jeffrey*** *with a chip in mid-air.*

Alex (To audience): Just look at them, (pause, then indicates) Lawrence - the one with the manbag, clipboard and the hair - he's the so-called Director. I say "so-called" because he couldn't direct his way out of a wet paper bag. (Stage whisper.) He's on the verge - spends a lot of his day in La-La Land. Bit of a mummy's boy - likes to shout - you know the sort - your boss is probably a bit like that. Then there's Bea, in charge of costumes - costumes! I mean, look at her! Got the fashion sense of Stevie Wonder. Lovely girl, though - caring. Got a degree in Media Studies from Huddersfield. A 2:2. Mind you, they give you one of those with a year's subscription to *Hello* magazine - so not the brightest in the firmament, but certainly knows who is knocking off who and who is doing what to who and what with - if you see what I mean. Then there's Jeffrey. A professional jobsworth. Spends more time on training courses than actually doing anything and he's the Health and Safety rep. So he spends more and more time doing less and less. Before long, he'll *know* absolutely everything and *do* absolutely nothing. *(Gestures towards **Poppy**.)* Poppy - poor Poppy. Spends a lot of time in the props loft with the leading man. It must be really hot up there, because they often come down with fewer clothes on than when they went up. She is our prompter - which would be fine if it weren't for the fact that she is dyslexic *and* short-sighted. She's okay if she has her lenses in and the script has little words in a big print. Anyway, Jeffrey is probably getting arm-ache so we'll get on with our story. I'll talk to you again later. I'm Alex by the way. *(Sarcastically.)* You could have read that in the programme if you had bought one.

*Spot fades, lights come up and everyone unfreezes. **Poppy** and **Bea** wander off, chatting. **Lawrence** looks at the unfinished cottage, looks disparagingly at **Jeffrey** and writes in his clipboard. He takes out his mobile phone and starts shouting as he exits.*

Lawrence *(Exiting)*: What? They can't be serious ... a Panda Bear? I do not believe it, I just don't believe it ...

__Alex__ takes a screwdriver to work on the beanstalk motor wiring.

Jeffrey *(Mimicking Lawrence)*: "I don't believe it, I just do not believe it"!

Jeffrey unravels one of the pages from his chip wrappings.

Alex: What don't you believe this time?

Jeffrey: It says 'ere that we are paying this bloke, this foreigner, his five kids and his missus, to stay in a posh flat in London and he's only gone and nicked some stuff from an old lady. We can't send him back because of his "human rights" - I just don't believe it! It also says that some other bloke couldn't be deported because he had bought a cat! A sodding cat! I ask you - place is definitely going to the dogs.

Alex: What's that you're reading then - PDSA Quarterly?

Jeffrey: Don't you try to be funny and, anyway, have you fixed the cottage yet?

Alex: Why should I do it? I'm busy doing this *(indicates complicated wiring).*

Jeffrey: Well, Lawrence won't be happy if it's not fixed. He had a go at me on Wednesday night but I told him - I don't do ladders - told him straight. I get nose-bleeds climbing to the top of a double-decker bus.

Sound effect - Steam Train.

Sound Box: Was that the right coach and horses sound?

Alex *(Together)*: }
Jeffrey: } NO!

Alex: I know he's new around here, but really! Now, remind me again, is it blue to earth, green, brown, or green stripey?

Jeffrey: Green - earth's green, well, it always used to be any road. I told him the "Work at Height Regulation", 2005 - says I must be over 18, trained and risk-assessed.

Alex: And one out of three wasn't good enough for him? ... You sure about green?

Jeffrey: I told you before, lay off the cheek, it's bad enough listening to madam without you having a go as well.

Alex puts down the electrical thing, moves SR and starts to put the remaining bits of the cottage, which wobbles, together.

Alex: She's not still going on about having to act in a pantomime is she?

Jeffrey *(Putting down paper)*: Going on? Going on? She thinks panto is somewhere below *Crossroads* and not much above *I'm A Celebrity ... Get Me Out of Here*. She says that at RADA they never taught her how to be cheap and vulgar. Type-casting if you ask me!

Alex: Well, I think it's time we did something a bit more modern - a bit more with it. Rather than the usual gloomy stuff - Chekov bores me to tears; and anyway, it'll do her good, letting her hair down. Even better - she has to play the Dame. Pity it's not the Wicked Witch of the West - now *that* would be type-casting.
Thunder and lightning effect.
Sound: Sorry, just testing.
Jeffrey *(Shouts)*: Is that for her grand entrance then, when she parks her broomstick?
Sound: It was supposed to be the sound of the magic beans growing.
Jeffrey: Yes, beans have that effect on me too.
Sound: Look, we're having all sorts of problems up here. There's only me and a muppet on some government training scheme. It would help if he could tell his right hand from his left!
Alex *(Moving back to Jeffrey)*: Seriously, though, it's all going to be a bit of a come-down for Jasmine. It's bad enough that she's ended up here - wasn't she in something in the West End?
Jeffrey: That's what she puts about. Really, she had a few minor roles at the West Grimsthorpe rep. I heard that the director thought that she was too inflexible.
Alex: What - she was rubbish on the casting couch?
Jeffrey: Well, maybe that as well, but that she could only really do posh voices.
Alex *(Sits)*: Her Widow Twanky should be a real treat for the kids then - *(with heavy sarcasm)* certain to pack 'em in is that! We'll have them all rolling in the aisles.
Jeffrey: At least Rupert is up for something a bit different.
Alex: Yes, I heard that as well - didn't Bea catch him at it with Poppy in the props loft?
Jeffrey: Poor cow. She thinks that he'll leave his wife and kids for her, but there's no chance. He knows which side of his

croissant is buttered, all right. It's his missus that's got the money. I can't see him giving up his posh car and his foreign holidays for poor little Poppy. No, I think she's just the flavour of the month. But at least he's willing to give the panto a go - I think he's scared that if the company fails, he'll have to spend more time at home with Amanda and the kids. I envy him having a family to go home to and what does he do but risk it all. *(Reads his newspaper the lonely hearts section.)* Here, listen to this lonely hearts ad: "Whore in the kitchen and chef in the bedroom - woman (47) with mixed priorities and GSOH seeks man who can toss a good salad!"

Alex: Still on the lonely hearts kick? Fancy having one more turn on the merry-go-round?

Jeffrey: Thought I'd have one more crack at it. I've not had a decent hot meal since the missus left me, nor anything else hot, for that matter. I've put one or two ads in myself - you know - "Male, athletic, GSOH, theatre critic, WLTM Female mid 40s etc."

Alex: You - athletic? You run out of breath opening a tin of sardines. The only truth in that is "theatre critic" - you haven't got a good word for anyone here. And what are these secret codes you put in? What does "GSOH" mean? Geriatric Sod Old Has-been?

Jeffrey: I've told you, cut out the cheek. Anyway, it means "Good Sense of Humour".

Alex: Well, you shouldn't put that in your ad. You're a miserable old git at the best of times! Here, let's have a look. *(Takes paper.)* What's "WLTM" mean? Women's Libber Terrifies Men?

Jeffrey *(Disdainfully)*: "Would Like to Meet", actually.

Alex: Does anybody put in an accurate description of themselves?

Jeffrey: Not really, you have to be able to read between the lines.

Alex: Here then, Sherlock, work some of these out. What does "curvy" mean?
Jeffrey: Fat.
Alex: "Cuddly"?
Jeffrey: Fat.
Alex: "Likes eating out"?
Jeffrey: Lazy and fat.
Alex: "Athletic"?
Jeffrey: No boobs.
Alex: "Contagious smile"?
Jeffrey: On a lot of medication.
Alex: Good grief, it's a minefield! Why do you bother, is it all worth it?
Jeffrey: Not really, but I don't meet any women on Health and Safety courses. Well, not as you'd call women any road. The last one I tried to chat up had a fifteen-point check list before she would even consider going beyond first base.
Alex: How far did you get then?
Jeffrey: I failed on point seven - "Not Safe Without Fluorescent Protective Gear".
Alex: Oh! What exactly do they mean by "Protective Gear"?
Jeffrey: Over-jackets and trousers and stuff.
Alex: Oh, I thought you meant ... You know!
Lawrence appears from the auditorium looking very harassed, clipboard in one hand, scattering papers, and mobile in the other.
Lawrence (*Into phone, attempting to pick up papers*): Is that Acme Stage Supplies? ... I want to speak to Roderick ... No, no, no, not Nigel ... Oh, sorry, Nigella now, is it? ... No, I want to speak to Chief Running Water not Little Drip ... At last, thank you! ... Roderick, yes, it's me, Lawrence ... Yes, now, listen here ... No, I said listen, if I'd wanted a pantomime panda bear I would have said so. Whoever heard of Daisy the sodding-Panda being sold

for a bag of beans? ... What? I don't care if you've got a job lot from the National! You're unbelievable! And where is the Golden Carriage? ... What? ... No, I can't paint a spare dog cart from *Les Miserables*! It just won't do - sort it out.

(*To **Jeff** and **Alex**.*) You two, if it's not too much trouble, do you think we could have this set ready before I lose the will to live? The cottage is still not finished, the place is covered in rubbish, the beanstalk needs sorting - it looks as much like a beanstalk as Graham Norton looks like Tarzan! Get it sorted! Thank you.

Lawrence disappears behind set.

Jeffrey (*Looking up from his paper*): Ooer, get him! I'm not rushing, that's when accidents happen. And, anyway, you need scaffolding to do all that. I don't do ladders, he knows that. It's all in the H and S manual and, anyway, we're entitled to a tea break. He'd have us working like slaves.

Alex: It would be nice if you could fit a bit of work in between mugs of tea - that cottage still looks dodgy to me.

Jeffrey: I'll get round to it, don't worry. Here, make yourself useful and help me with the crossword. (*Looking at the newspaper.*) What's another word for "synonym"?

Alex: What? What are you on about? Look, if I go up the ladder, you can pass me some more of the green stuff for the beanstalk - if it's not too much trouble?

Jeffrey: All right, all right, keep your hair on. (*Gets up grudgingly.*) Oh, my poor knees, not very good as knees.

Alex: What are they good for then?

Alex goes up ladder with beanstalk material and attaches a few leaves to stalk.

Jeffrey: Well, not for going up ladders, that's for sure. Here. (*Throws more greenery up.*) Let's hope wonder boy is happy with his magic beanstalk. (*He goes to pull the string, attached to the motor which raises the beanstalk - a fairly droopy, pathetic specimen.*) What do you think, then? Will the magic effect have them gasping with wonderment in the aisles? Will the children be wetting themselves with excitement? Will the critics be comparing the magic beanstalk to the flying car in *Chitty Chitty Bang Bang*?

Alex: Well, the word "Chitty" certainly springs to mind. Look, I know we're short on cash, but if this is the best we can do for special effects, then we might as well start looking in the job vacancies in *The Stage*, or in the local rag for Career Opportunities at *McDonald's*. *(Looks round, moves to centre of stage.)* How on earth did we end up here, eh? Did you always want to work in the theatre?

Jeffrey: No, I sort of drifted into it, really. I started off doing casual work when I lost my job at the undertakers.

Alex *(Sarcastically)*: How did you lose your job - too cheerful an attitude, perhaps? Too much the Happy chappie? Here, give us a hand!

Jeffrey *(Holds cottage flat, but doesn't actually do anything)*: Sarky sod! I've told you - lay off! No, there was a misunderstanding with some bloke's missus.

Alex: You weren't trying to pick her up, were you?

Jeffrey: No, just the opposite - I dropped her. I tripped on some loose gravel and her coffin slipped out of my hand and landed on the vicar's foot. He said a few words which don't generally feature in a funeral service and I got my marching orders from the boss: "Onward Christian Soldiers", "Go forth and multiply" - you know the sort of thing.

Alex *(Getting somewhere with the cottage)*: Pity, a steady job that, easy to get to - dead centre of the town.

Jeffrey: You're not funny. I wasn't that bothered, really. They didn't take Health and Safety seriously. She was a big woman - I reckon they should have used a fork-lift truck to cart her off - it's what did for my back, you know!

Alex: You can't use a fork-lift truck - it's not respectful and it wouldn't fit down the aisle. Anyway, you're not going to last here much longer if you're not careful. I heard Lawrence talking to the Finance bloke about cutting staff and your name was mentioned, something about you not being very good value for money - too bothered about rules.

Jeffrey: That's just typical, isn't it? Here am I, taking an active interest in everyone's welfare, and that's the thanks I get. Bloody typical! I'll show them, they can't sack me. I'll get Equity on to them.

Alex: You're joking, they won't help, there's far too many members out of work to bother defending someone like you. You haven't got a hope. If I were you, I would start looking seriously in the jobs section.

Jeffrey lets go of the cottage, leaving Alex to carry on, on his own. Cottage wobbles, but stays up. Jeffrey sits down and picks up paper.

Jeffrey: It says here in my horoscope that I'm going to have a great opportunity soon to break away from the common herd and be able to be my true self!!

Alex *(Moves over to Jeffrey, looks over his shoulder)*: What sign are you, then?

Jeffrey: Taurus.

Alex: Ah! That helps explain all the bullshit!! What does mine say, then?

Jeffrey: When's your birthday?

Alex: January 1st - Capricorn.

Jeffrey: Your mother certainly knew how to start the New Year with a good clear out! Let's have a look ... Capricorn, here we are: "Be confident this week when making decisions - they'll be wrong, but make them with gusto! A good week to wear a disguise."

Alex: Go on, you're having me on!

Jeffrey: No, honest, straight up, would I lie to you?

Lawrence enters, agitated.

Lawrence: Are you two still wasting time? I've got a show to put on and would appreciate it if you could get off your backsides and actually do something. I've got a delivery of dry-ice coming and I need you to get down to the goods entrance and sort it, then store it safely in the freezer room.

Alex *(To Jeffrey)*: I've still got this bit of painting to finish off - can you make yourself useful for a change?

Jeffrey: I can't be expected to do all that lifting on my own. Regulations state that at all times management shall ensure that ...

Lawrence: All right, you've made your point, I'll see if I can find someone to help you. *(Shouts off.)* Poppy! *(Louder.)* Poppy!!

Alex: She's probably up in the props loft *(looks knowingly at Jeffrey)*, having a rummage round with Rupert.

Lawrence: Oh, what again? I don't know what she finds to do up there, I'll see if Bea can help, *(shouts)* Bea!!

Bea *(With attitude from off)*: What?! *(She enters carrying various props/costumes.)* What is it, now? I'm busy. I'm having to make do with these old costumes until you manage to sort out the suppliers. Have you ever thought of paying their bill?

Lawrence: I have rung them, but they are not being very cooperative. Look, can you lend a hand here, we need the dry-ice putting away in the freezer and Jeffrey can't manage it all on his own.

Bea: Well, I feel sorry for him, but I've got enough to do without going down there with him.

Lawrence *(Taking her arm, moving downstage)*: Look, pretty please, can you just go and help him for a few minutes, I need to explain to those clowns in the lighting and sound box the difference between play and fast forward on the sound deck.

Sound: We heard that!!

Blackout. Thunder and lightning effect.

Lawrence: Sorry! Sorry! Please put the lights back on, I didn't mean it; we are just a bit stressed down here.

Sound: You're stressed? You should try working in here. This equipment is out of the Ark. The only thing digital in here is my finger and that's what you'll get if you don't get off my case.

Lights flicker back on.

Lawrence: Look, I said I was sorry, didn't I? Can we just get on? ... All I want to do is to put on a little pantomime - is that asking too much?

Sound: And while I'm at it, it's like a sauna in here, it's far too hot. It's no wonder the equipment keeps breaking down.

Jeffrey: Really? You should come and talk to me! According to "The Workplace (Health, Safety and Welfare) Regulations 1992" you should be provided with, and I quote, "Suitable clothing or means of cooling". Have you got air conditioning up there? Or beach shorts and flip flops?

Sound: Air conditioning? We haven't got even a packet of cool mints! I've got sweat dripping down my neck.

Lawrence: Well, I've got the perfect solution, you come down out of your sweat box and go with Jeffrey and Bea to put away the dry-ice in the freezer. How about that?

Sound: You're all heart. Okay, I'm on my way.

Jeffrey: Well in that case, I will go. I've got some brochures you can look at concerning working conditions. It's time that the management starting taking our welfare seriously. Perhaps a work to rule is called for?

Lawrence (*Exasperatedly*): That's all I need, a work to rule. Mind you, even if you went on strike, I don't think anyone would notice the difference.

Jeffrey: Sarcasm is the lowest form of wit. That could be construed as bullying in the workplace. There are laws about that, too. I could take you to a tribunal, you know. Come on, Bea, let's get it shifted. *(Turns back to Lawrence.)* Where are the special gloves? I'm not handling dry-ice without gloves. You can get frostbite, you know.

Bea: I've got some gloves from the props box. We used them in *The Ice Maiden*. They will have to do you.

Jeffrey: I'll just need to check in the safety manual, I've never worked in a freezer before.

Bea: I tell you what, I'll go inside the freezer - you just pass the blocks to me, how about that?

Jeffrey *(Exiting)*: I'm still not sure about this. I'm being treated like a general dogsbody.

Bea *(Pushing him off the set)*: And they call women the weaker sex!

Alex: I think you're being a bit hard on him. I know he goes on a bit, but he does have everyone's interests at heart, really.

Lawrence: I think Health and Safety has got a lot to answer for. Single-handedly, it has stopped us being competitive with just about everyone - even Belgium. It's costing us a fortune. Did you know we have to hire scaffolding to change a light bulb now? You don't think other countries bother like we do, do you?

Alex: Probably not.

Lawrence: I always think that if the Health and Safety rep is seen but not heard, then it's a shame to wake him!

Alex: Talking about lighting, I've got one for you - how many safety managers does it take to screw in a light bulb?

Lawrence: I don't know - go on.

Alex: One. The safety manager holds it, while the Earth revolves around him!

Lawrence: Very good. I was always told that the only difference between a safety manager and God is that God doesn't think he's a safety manager!

Alex: That sums Jeffrey up nicely.

Bea (*Off, increasingly exasperatedly*)**:** Don't sit on that! Ooh, that's going to be painful. Mind where you put that! Well, give it a good rub then!!

Lawrence: Oh, good grief, what now? Look, I've got more phone calls to make, you finish up here, will you?

Lawrence exits.

Alex (*Alone, paintbrush in hand, looks round to see if anyone is listening, moves into spotlight, the rest of the set darkens slightly*)**:**
"O Romeo, Romeo, wherefore art thou Romeo?
Deny thy father and refuse thy name;
Or if thou wilt not, be but sworn my love
And I'll no longer be a Capulet.
'Tis but thy name that is my enemy."
(**Bea** *just about to walk on, stops, listens quietly for a few moments, then slips away.*)
"What's in a name? That which we call a rose
By any other word would smell as sweet;"
(*Sighs.*) Who am I kidding? Me, an actor? What do I know about acting? Back to the painting, I suppose.

Lights fade to black out.

Curtain

Scene Two

Rupert is on stage with script practicing lines.

Rupert: "If you can't pay the rent you, I will have my men evict you, so stop your snivelling and" ... Oh bugger, what is it? *(Looks at script.)* Oh, yes, "start packing, and take that idiot boy of yours with you."
Repeats last line twice, trying it with different theatrical voices.
Poppy enters.
Poppy *(Moving towards Rupert)*: Rupi - where were you last night? You said that you would come round, I waited up for ages ... I got you your favourite - steak and some Pinot Noir, why didn't you come?
Rupert *(Moving away from her)*: Sorry, darling, couldn't get away. Flossie had a temperature so that she couldn't go to her "Kick-boxing for Princesses" club and Amanda had to go to her Tai Chi lessons - it was far too late when she got back in.
Poppy: That's not much of an excuse - couldn't you have taken the dog for a walk or something, or gone jogging like any normal adulterer? It wasn't that long ago when you would have used any excuse to get away - you couldn't wait to get your paws on me. I seem to remember you were all over me when we were rehearsing the Chekov. I'm sure that Bea saw us in the props loft that time - when you told her you were looking for a stuffed seagull - I don't think she believed you.
Rupert: I have to be really careful, it's difficult phoning and texting you, I'm sure that she checks up on my phone calls, and I'm running out of excuses to text you about things to do with the play.
Poppy: I told you to get another SIM card, one of those "Pay As You Go" jobs, then all you have to do is swap the card

when you want to make an arrangement - or *cancel* one. Look, pass me your phone and I'll show you. *(She takes SIM card out of her phone and swaps it into his. Note: A piece of plastic Velcro taped to the back of each phone is convincing.)* There, it's as simple as that, even an idiot like you could do it. Now you swap them back.

Rupert: You know I struggle with all of these phones and pads and stuff - I rely on the kids to sort out anything technological. *(As he is swapping them back, he drops the SIM cards, muddling them up.)* I can't seem to get anything right these days. Amanda won't even trust me to put up some shelves. She called in Steve, the local handyman, to put together something that we bought from IKEA - KLAPDIM it was called - rather appropriately I thought. I couldn't make head nor tail of the diagrams before I even started. So she said that she would have to call a man in, with rather too much emphasis on the word "man" for my liking.

Poppy *(Moves away, becoming increasingly assertive as the scene progresses)***:** You need to stand up to her, tell her that you are not happy and that you are going to leave.

Rupert *(Approaches her)***:** You know it's not as simple as that. I can't just up sticks and go - I can't afford to! Everything's in her name - the house, the time-share, even the car is leased from Daddies' company.

Poppy *(Pointing finger at Rupert)***:** You know what I think? I think that you are just looking for any old excuse to back out, but you haven't got the guts to say so.

Rupert: Poppy, precious ... I don't ...

Poppy *(Pointing)***:** Don't you dare patronise me. I've gone along with your excuses and it's about time to face up to a few things. I'm looking for the payback on some of the promises you've made me - what about the weekend away? Have you even booked that yet?

Rupert: Look, it's not that easy. Amanda keeps a sharp eye on what I spend. She looks at all the bank statements and she pays most of the bills - I even have to get the garage to put my cigarettes on to the account as fuel. It's the only Honda that does less than 20 to the gallon!

Poppy: It's just one excuse after another! You're pathetic, Rupert, just pathetic! I've gone along with all of the secrecy for the sake of Flossie. Poor kid doesn't deserve to be messed around, but I've just about had enough. *(Turning away.)* Oh, look out, here's God's gift to thespians everywhere.

Jasmine enters stage right.

Jasmine: Daahlings - not interrupting anything am I? Not having a teensy tiff?

Poppy: Don't know what you mean. *(Under breath.)* Nosey cow.

Rupert: What are you suggesting, Jasmine? We were just having a private conversation.

Jasmine *(Standing between them)***:** Oh, come on, you two - everyone knows what you're up to. You weren't very private up in the props loft, were you? According to Bea you were being very inventive with the stuff from the Agatha Christie we did two years ago - the one with the truncheon and the handcuffs? And, anyway, it doesn't take a genius to work out what's going on - you're always sneaking off together and that designer perfume of yours is rather distinctive, daahling Popsie. A bit like cat pee on a warm blanket! I can always tell when he's been around you!

Poppy: Bitch!

Jas'e: Oh, come on, Popsie, do try to be a big girl. We all know what he's like. There aren't any of us he hasn't tried it on with. Even I had a little thing with him a few years back - before he married Amanda. But, to be honest, daahling, he's not really worth it. *(Looks at **Rupert** disparagingly.)* All mouth and no trousers, if you get my drift.

Rupert *(Turns to Jasmine angrily)*: That was a bit below the belt! If I remember rightly, you were the one who did all of the running.

Jasmine: And If I remember rightly, daahling, you struggled to keep up with me - a bit like one of those vintage cars. You sort of ran out of steam when a bit of extra push was needed *(mimes a pelvic thrust)*. Anyway, fortunately for me, I only have to act that I like you on stage.

Rupert: Oh, Jazz, you know I actually cared for you once, but you've become really bitter - the failure of the years is becoming etched in your face and it's poisoning you.

Jasmine: At least I have got some glory days to look back on - I worked with Larry, you know. He said that my interpretation of a Weird Sister in *Macbeth* was unforgettable! *(Strikes a theatrical pose.)* "Fair is foul, and foul is fair: Hover through the fog and filthy air; Double, double, toil and trouble." The only memorable thing said about you was when the *Neasden Courier* said your Richard the Third had delusions of adequacy.

Rupert: You really are becoming a sad old bore. All the vicious lines you've spouted are gathering around your neck, *(strokes her neck, Jasmine reacts)* daaaahling!

Poppy: Come on you two, pack it in. We've got to work together on this, if we can't make a go of this pantomime and make some cash, then the company is finished.

Jasmine *(Starting to move away)*: You're quite right, Popsie daahling. It's not worth the effort with him, as I'm sure you are finding out. *(To Rupert.)* I only came along to tell you that Lawrence has decided that he wants us to try out some of the ghastly costumes for the rehearsal, with some of the technical stuff as well. So, if you've finished with your bit of fluff, you had better get your skates on. You don't want to keep his lordship waiting. Bye.
Jasmine flounces off.

Poppy: "Double double, toil and trouble" - bitch! "Hovering through the fog and filthy air" - double double bitch! She just spreads trouble wherever she goes. *(Turning on Rupert.)* And don't think I've finished with you yet - weasel!

Rupert *(Sulkily)*: You don't need to take it out on me - I don't deserve any of this.

Poppy *(Facing up to Rupert)*: Don't deserve? Don't deserve? You deserve everything that's coming to you. *(Pokes him in the chest.)* I'm fed up of making all of the running! It's time to grow a backbone and stand up for yourself - you know, actually make a decision for once!

Rupert: Look, Poppy, it was fun while it lasted, but it's all getting a bit too heavy. I do like you - a lot, but, to be honest, I don't think it's going to work out.

Poppy: You bastard! I *knew* you wouldn't leave her! You just don't have the guts, do you? So it all comes down to money, does it? After all you've said about her, you're crawling back to Amanda. You can't manage without your pocket money, you poor little kept boy! So it's true what Jasmine said then - you talk big, but when it comes to it, that's all there is - talk, wind. A bit like an old fart, really, you hang around and you're unpleasant.

Rupert: Poppy, don't be like that! We can still meet up, still have some fun ...

Jasmine is seen quietly watching from the side of the stage.

Poppy *(Pacing)*: You just don't get it, do you? I'm looking for commitment, my biological clock is winding down - I want a family, security. You know, a *home* together. I was prepared to sacrifice material things just to be with you, but I've put up with the furtive meetings and the whisperings for long enough. I've had it with you, Rupert. You can clear off back to Amanda *(runs off, sobbing)* - she's welcome to you!

Rupert *(Shouts after her)*: It's no good trying to talk to you, you are just being irrational! *(Door slams off. To himself, bitterly.)* And another one bites the dust. *(Sees Jasmine watching, moves to centre stage.)* Come to gloat, have you? Come to put the boot in?

Jasmine: Not really, but that would be fun. No, I came to see what all the fuss was about and Lawrence is getting really rather agitated. I think he's losing the plot - it's all getting too much for him. I mean, it strikes of desperation agreeing to put on a pantomime in my view.

Rupert: He's not the only one. I just can't seem to get it right, no matter what I do. My wife treats me with contempt, Poppy has just blown me out and even the dog growls at me when I try to take him for a walk. And here I am, in a second-rate rep company, reduced to playing the Evil Baron in a pantomime. Pretty pathetic, really.

Jasmine: Oh no, you're not!

Rupert: Oh yes, I a ... Oh God, just listen to me! I'm turning into a Pantomime.

Jasmine: Well, as reluctant as I am to say this, you've got to put your mind back into work. Lawrence's fuse is getting shorter by the minute and he wants us to get ready now. You know, the show must go on and all that.

Rupert *(Sits, with head in hands)*: I can't really concentrate on my words at the moment, my life is in such a mess. The hours we work mean that I hardly ever see the kids. I missed another parents' evening for Flossie last week, Amanda went on her own and I'm sure that the teacher thinks we are separated. She kept making hints about "is everything all right at home?"

Jasmine *(Sits with him)*: But you have only yourself to blame - you shouldn't go playing away. Women have a way of sensing these things, unless they choose to ignore it or are totally stupid and I don't think Amanda is stupid. Mind you, she did marry you.

Rupert *(Jumps to his feet)*: But I need something that she just can't give me. She just doesn't understand what a solitary life it is being an actor - the adrenaline high that you get from performing - it's almost like being on drugs. I can never get to sleep for hours after a show, especially if things have gone really well - or badly for that matter. I get home late, especially if we have gone for a drink afterwards, and she's always in bed. She gets up early to get the girls to school and to get herself to work. We sleep in separate bedrooms and so, altogether, our social life and our sex life are practically zero.

Jasmine *(Sympathetically, indicating for Rupert to sit down)*: Does Amanda have to work, I thought she was loaded?

Rupert *(Sits again)*: She works for her Father. He's the one with the money. He owns a double-glazing company, wanted me to go into the business: "great opportunities in sales for someone with the gift of the gab"; "you could make sales manager eventually"! *(Groans.)* I have resorted to working for him part-time when I've been resting, but it's so *soul* destroying. I'd rather watch paint dry, or even do *Waiting for Godot* for that matter.

Jasmine: So how come you ended up marrying her after we split up?

Rupert: It was a classic case of marrying on the rebound - that and the offer of a house and car provided by *Daddy*. My actor's wages were never going to stretch far enough to get a mortgage. You know what it's like when you go for a loan and you say to the bank manager that you are an actor. It's like someone with leprosy wanting a job in Tesco's - you are on the opposite side of the door before you can say zero collateral!

Jasmine: Yes, I was lucky there. I had a trust fund which paid out when I was twenty-one. I never had to bother too much about money, although it's beginning to run out a bit now. You would have been much better off with me - missed your big chance there, didn't you?

Rupert: To quote Joni Mitchell "you don't know what you've got 'til it's gone."

The song "Let's Face the Music and Dance" is heard in the background.

Jasmine: Come on, trouper - that's our cue. *(Mimes little dance routine.)* Let's get this charade on the road and get it over with.

Rupert: Yes, I suppose we had better "face the music and dance".

They exit dancing. Music gets louder as curtain closes.

Scene Three

*Curtain opens to reveal **Lawrence** downstage or in the auditorium. **Poppy** is sitting stage left with prompt book, knitting and a large box of tissues. She clearly has been crying. **Jeff** and **Alex** are tidying up/finishing off painting. The cottage is completed, but looks dodgy.*

Lawrence *(To everyone in general)*: We're going to try this scene without books, but with sound and lighting effects. I don't hold out a lot of hope of seeing anything remotely artistic, judging by what I saw at yesterday's rehearsal, but you never know. We'll go from the scene where the Baron comes in to demand his rent money. Now, has anyone seen Brian and Derek? They were supposed to be practicing with the Ermintrude costume. Bea, have you seen them? ... Bea? ... Has anyone seen Bea?

Alex *(To Sound)*: Didn't you go down to the cold store with her to put away the dry ice?

Sound: Yes, but I left Jeffrey with her to finish up after carrying in the boxes. I went off for a cup of tea.

Jeffrey *(Goes pale)*: Oh my God! The catch on the door is faulty! I was supposed to go back for her to let her out. British Standards "Ergonomics of the Thermal Environment" says that she should only be in there for 20 minutes and she should have thermal underwear on - I bet she hasn't. Oh, if she's got frostbite anywhere, I'll have to file a report! Oh, what would I write? Oh, the paperwork, the paperwork *(rushes off)* ...

Alex: I think he can expect a frosty reaction when he gets there!

Lawrence *(Glares at Alex)*: It's bad enough that he doesn't do any work, never mind trying to kill off Bea - I hope she's all right! *(Sounds offstage of a furious row between Bea and Jeffrey. Shouting off.)* Bea!!

Bea *(Poking her head round a flat, with attitude)*: What!!

Lawrence *(Exasperatedly)*: I'm trying to direct a rehearsal here! Where is everyone? ... Where's my cow? My Cow?

Alex *(Impression of Olivier)*: My kingdom for a cow!

Lawrence gives Alex a withering look.

Bea *(Enters, looking very cold, clutching a hot water bottle)*: I was left in the freezer for 20 minutes and all you are interested in is your sodding cow?!

Jeffrey creeps in guiltily.

Lawrence *(Attempting to placate)*: Look, love, I'm sorry that you got left in the freezer and I'm really sorry that you didn't have your... you know... thermal knickers on... but I need my cow now!! This place is like the Marie Celeste!

Bea *(Still shivering)*: Well, actually, it's more like the Titanic, really - appropriate we have all that ice - plenty enough to sink all of us. Apparently, Brian and Derek have had a better offer from the Playhouse - a guaranteed contract and more money - and so they have downed costume and hoofed it *(snigger)*.

Lawrence *(Bitterly)*: There's loyalty for you! Where am I going to get two halves of a pantomime cow at such short notice?

Bea: They are doing *Aladdin* at the Playhouse and they needed two wash-house workers for the slapstick scene and Brian said that getting covered in soapy water and Widow Twankey's wet bras and bloomers every night was a step up the career ladder, compared with being the back end of a cow. Apparently, Derek's diet of curried beans was making his position untenable.

Lawrence *(Not realising what he is saying)*: Well, I never got wind of the fact that they were going. I suppose I'll have to fill in the part of the cow for now, just so that we can get the rehearsal started. Bea, can you check on the cow costume, please? Make sure that the suppliers haven't substituted it for some other exotic animal - a pantomime lizard maybe.

Bea: Anything to get warm!
Bea glares pointedly at Jeffrey and exits.
Lawrence: Right. *(Shouting to offstage.)* Baron and Dame, Act I, Scene Two, positions please! *(Pause.)* Sometime today, if that's not too inconvenient!
Jasmine *(Off)*: I'm having trouble getting my bloomers on.
Jeffrey *(To Alex)*: She normally gets 'em off quickly enough!
Sound *(Off)*: Can I try out some entrance music while we're waiting?
Lawrence: Only if you can get it marginally correct and roughly at the right time. Right, positions please!
Rupert and Jasmine enter as the Evil Squire and Dame, respectively - have fun with their costumes!
Jasmine: Say one word and that's it, I'll leave! I've never felt so ridiculous in all of my life.
Lawrence *(Wearily)*: This is the scene where Jack has to take Ermintrude to the market because they can't pay the rent. We are going to try it without scripts, if you please. Are you okay with that, Poppy?
Poppy *(Puts down knitting and stands)*: I suppose so. But I'm not at my best today, Lawrence, you will just have to bear with me. I've had to take my contacts out. *(Glaring at Rupert.)* You could say that I have had a *pig* of a day!
Poppy sits down again.
Lawrence: Well, just do your best. Okay, positions please. Cue music! *(Nothing happens.)* Cue music!!
Totally inappropriate music is heard, eg World War II battle sounds.
Sound: Sorry!
Lawrence *(Throws clipboard on the floor in a tantrum)*: For crying out loud! Is it too much to ask - we want music representing a rural pantomime scene, not a re-enactment of Pearl Harbour! Just for once, can you lot get your act together - it's not rocket science!
Rupert and Jasmine: sharp intake of breath - "Oooohh!"
Eventually, after a few false starts, appropriate music plays.

Lawrence: Thank you. Right, let's try again. Rupert, sorry, Squire Blackheart, you enter from stage right. Dame, you are over there. I'm the cow, tied up outside.
Lawrence moves stage left, looks at script on clipboard.

Rupert *(Knocks on Dame's cottage door - sound FX of knocking)***:** I know you're in there. It's no use hiding. I've come for my rent. I've been far too lenient with you, but if you can't pay you will be out on your ear - both you and that waste of space of a son of yours!

Jasmine *(In a very posh voice)***:** Oh, have mercy on me, for I cannot pay the rent! I am but a poor widow woman who has fallen on hard times!

Lawrence *(In amazement)***:** What do you think you are doing? This is supposed to be a pantomime, not flipping Brecht! You are supposed to be a homely peasant woman. You want the audience to feel some sympathy towards your plight. You are sounding like some posh totty who is having to make do with last year's Gucci handbag! Now try to act the part.

Jasmine: One tries one's best, but it's hard associating oneself with the hoi polloi.

Lawrence: Well, please try a lot harder! I thought you trained at RADA - didn't they teach you character acting?

Jasmine: I've worked with Sir Larry and Sir John and they never treated me like this.

Lawrence *(Increasingly hysterical)***:** Well, now you are working with me, for the time being, and I want you to act as a pantomime Dame, so, if it's not too much trouble, can we please get on with the rehearsal? Right, Squire, from your entrance, please.

Rupert *(Knocks on cottage door - different sound FX, Rupert glares at Sound)***:** I know you're in there. It's no use hiding. I've come for my rent. I've been far too lenient with you, but if you can't pay you will be out on your ear - both you and that waste of space of a son of yours!

Jasmine *(With exaggerated varying accents)*: Oh, Lordy, Lordy! Have mercy on me, for I canna pay the rent! I am but a poor widder woman who has fell on 'ard times!
Lawrence *(Stunned silence - looks on in disbelief)*: What the f...?
Poppy *(Suppressing giggles)*: That's not exactly as in the script.
Alex: Sounds like a bad production of *Tom Sawyer* played by a manic Scottish pirate.
Jeffrey *(With false Scottish pirate accent)*: Well, if she carries on like this, we're all doomed, I tells thee. Doomed!
Rupert *(Takes Jasmine to one side)*: Look, love, we both know that you were brought up in Barnsley, so cut out the posh bint accent and try acting. I don't want to do a pantomime either, but the way things are going, we don't have any choice, do we?
Jasmine *(Resignedly)*: I'll try, but only because you asked me ...
Lawrence: Right, again please - places.
Correct music - everyone looks in astonishment at Sound.
Poppy *(Stands, to Rupert)*: Cue: "I know you're in there ..."
Rupert: I know, I know! I was just composing myself ...
Poppy *(Impatiently)*: Well, I can't tell the difference, it sounded like you had forgotten your words *(scathingly)* ... perhaps more stage fright?
Rupert: If I need a prompt, I'll ask for it, all right?
Poppy *(With venom)*: Right!
Poppy sits with her back to Rupert.
Rupert *(Knocks on Dame's cottage door - sound FX of door bell - reaction from Rupert)*: I know you're in there! It's no use hiding. I've come for my rent. I've been far too lenient with you, but if you can't pay you will be out on your ear - both you and that waste of space of a son of yours!
Jasmine *(Enters through cottage door which wobbles alarmingly, with a brave attempt at a common voice)*: Oh, have mercy on me, for I cannot pay the rent! I am but

a poor widow woman who has fallen on hard times! Oh, if only Jack could find a rich girl to marry, that's the only way he will get any money - certainly not by working. He's been on the dole so long, they've put him on their permanent staff.

Rupert: Enough of your snivelling. I want my rent. If I don't get my thirty shiny gold coins, I will send round my men to evict you. And if I'm in a bad mood, I'll get them to duff you up a bit as well, just to cheer myself up. *(Jeffrey and Alex - "Boo!" To the audience.)* And you lot can shut up as well. I'll be back later, have my rent money ready or else its curtains for both of you!

Rupert exits to boos.

Jasmine (*Sobbing*): Oh, what shall become of me and Jack? *(Blows nose on unfeasibly large handkerchief.)* Ever since I lost my husband I've been a poor widow woman, taking in a bit of washing, doing a bit of this and a bit of that. I tried a bit of the other, but I couldn't get the hang of it - I always seemed to end up paying somehow! Oh, Ermintrude, I know you're only a cow, but you are the only friend I've got! Can you tell me what to do?

Silence.

Poppy: Cue: "Moo!" Lawrence, you said that you would take Ermintrude's part!

Lawrence (*Throwing a tantrum*): It's no good! I can't do everything! It's just too much! I can't direct, sort that lot out *(indicating Sound)*, do battle with the suppliers *and* act as well! *(To Alex and Jeffrey.)* I don't suppose you two could make yourselves useful for a little while and take the part of Ermintrude?

Jeffrey: On yer bike! We're not actors, you know! No, we're craftsmen! There's nothing in my contract about acting.

Alex (*Quietly to Jeffrey*): If we agree to do this for him, he might not be so ready to get rid of you.

Jeffrey: But I can't act! I'll get stage fright and probably forget my words!

Alex: What words? All we have to say is "Moo", for God's sake. I'll take the lead if that bothers you and then all you'll have to do is grab hold of my waist and follow what I do; and it might just be enough to save your job.

Jeffrey: All right, all right! I'll do it, I'll do it. But I'm going to check up on the Union regulations about how long I'm supposed to be inside that costume with you - and I bet it'll play havoc with my back *and*, while I think of it, what's the costume made of? I might be allergic to it ...

Lawrence: Oh, for crying out loud, I wish I'd never asked!

Alex: It's all right, don't worry, he's like this about everything, we'll get the costume on *(shouts off)* ... Bea!

Bea *(Off, with attitude)*: What now?! *(Appears, now wrapped in a duvet, hot water bottles strapped around her waist as well.)* I'm still trying to get warm after *he (indicates Jeffrey)* left me stuck in the freezer.

Alex: Can you get the old Ermintrude costume out for us? Jeff and I are going to act as the cow for the time being.

Bea: You are joking, aren't you? You're far too big to fit into that costume and I've spent ages sorting it out, curling the eyelashes, buffing up the horns and polishing the udders.

Jeffrey *(To Jasmine)*: That's what you've been doing all morning to get ready, isn't it?

Rupert quietly re-enters.

Jasmine: How dare you! You despicable little man, don't you dare speak to me like that. Lawrence, tell him that he can't speak to me like that ... go on tell him.

Lawrence: Er ... well ... I er ...

Jasmine: Typical. You men are all the same - spineless! *(To Rupert.)* Poppy is right, you are pathetic. You're all innuendo, with not much emphasis on the "do". *(To Jeffrey.)* And *you*, all *you* can do is make sarcastic com-

ments and avoid doing any real work. *(To **Lawrence**, who by now is a crumpled wreck.)* And as for *you*, I don't think you could direct yourself down a one-way street! I don't think you've got a cat in hell's chance of getting this pantomime off the ground. You'll find me in the Green Room when you are all finally ready to rehearse!
Jasmine storms off. Stunned silence.

Alex: Does that mean she thinks I'm okay then?

Jasmine *(Off)*: No!

Alex *(Looks crestfallen)*: Oh.

Bea: Think I'll ... er ... just go and get the costume then. Won't be a minute.

Bea exits.

Rupert: Think I'll ... er ... just go and powder my wig, won't be long.

Poppy *(Sarcastically)*: Missing you already. Oh, I suppose I'd better go and see how Madam is, see if I can't calm her down a bit.

Poppy exits.

Lawrence: That wasn't exactly helpful, now was it, Jeff?

Jeffrey: I can't help it if she hasn't got a sense of humour. Mind you, I didn't expect her to go off on one like that. I know she hates the idea of being in a panto, but she doesn't have to take it out on us, does she?

Lawrence: I need her to do this and we can't afford to get anyone else. If we don't get this show on the road, we are all finished - the end of the road, in fact. The Financial Director is constantly on at me to make savings and to improve our audiences! I can't have you upsetting everyone the way you do. If you don't make much more of an effort, I'll have to let you go.

Jeffrey: So that's the way it is, is it? The way the cookie crumbles? You haven't the guts to get rid of her, so you pick on me. So what have I done, then?

Lawrence: Well, that's the whole point really: not very much, apart from being lazy, incompetent, belligerent, obstructive, nit-picking ... Do you want me to go on?

Jeffrey *(Slumps)*: Not really - I get the picture.

Lawrence: But it might not come to that, if we can all just pull together and act as a team, we might just pull it off. Now, how about this rehearsal - you two will have a go at being Ermintrude, just until I can get hold of the Agency?

Alex *(Moves upstage)*: Come on Jeff, could be fun!

Jeffrey: I've already said I'll give it a go, haven't I?

Bea *(Enters, bringing in the 2 halves of the cow, which has seen better days)*: Here she is. She's going to be a tight fit, just be careful with her. Who's the front end and who is the back end?

Alex *(Sniggers)*: I'll take the front, Jeff's more suited to being the back end.

Jeffrey: Watch it, you! Now, how does it fit *(examines udders)* ... what on Earth?!

Business putting costume on, Bea helping wherever possible. During the closing of the gap, which needs to be Velcro, lots of comments such as "Mind where you're putting your hand"; "Your hands are cold"; "Smells like someone died in here"; "Come on, it's not for heifer"; "Get your hands off my udders" etc.

Bea: That's the best I can do for now. I'll leave you to it, I've got to let out Madam's ball gown for the finale.

Bea exits.

Lawrence: Right, let me have a look at you. *(Cow moves to centre stage, at an angle.)* Well, you wouldn't win any prizes at the county show! Still, at least we're making some progress, at last. Now, while we're waiting for Jasmine to come back, I just want to try out some ideas for the panto. Dame Goodbody has to teach Ermintrude some tricks to make her more valuable to sell. So you have to say "Moo" at the right time, then you have to do a little dance. Let's try some questions.

Alex: Righto, sorry, I mean Moo!

Lawrence *(Shouts off)***:** Poppy, can you read out the Dame's part? ... Poppy? Where's she got to now?

Alex: Moooo!

Lawrence: What? What do you mean "Moo"!

Alex *(Shouting through costume head)***:** You said to answer Moo to all of your questions to show how clever I am.

Lawrence: I don't mean yet. *(Total exasperation.)* Good grief, I'm surrounded by them!

Alex *(Sorrowfully)***:** Mooo?

Lawrence: Look, do you or don't you know where Poppy is? And if you say moo again, I'll give you a good kicking in your udders.

Jeffrey *(Sticking head out of costume)***:** I'll report you to the RSPCA! *(Severe glare from Lawrence, so pulls head back under.)* Sorry.

Alex *(Muffled)***:** She followed Jasmine to get a drink.

Lawrence: What was that? The has-been has gone to see a shrink?

Alex: Nooo!

Jeffrey and Alex each wave their left leg, pointing towards the Green Room.

Lawrence: Oh yes, the Green Room. *(Mimes having a drink.)* I suppose I'll have to read in until they get back. Right, back to the plot. Now, Ermintrude, you stand here. *(Ermintrude attempts to move to allotted space, but there is a lack of co-ordination between the two halves.)* That looks awful, there's no co-ordination at all, you've got to work as a team.

Alex *(To Jeffrey)***:** Try this, follow my lead, when I say left, you walk with your left foot and vice versa. Try it - left, right, left, right.

This results in a very ungainly walk.

Lawrence: That's no good at all! It looks like some sort of deformed penguin! You need to take alternate steps.

Alex: Okay. When I say left, you go right, right?
Jeffrey: And when you say right, I go left, right?
Alex: Right. *(Jeffrey moves left leg, almost falling over.)* What are you doing?
Jeffrey: You said right, so I moved my left leg like you said.
Alex: I was just agreeing with you, not telling you to move!
Lawrence: Look, how about saying something like "Move, left, right" and so on?
Alex: I'll try it and see how it goes I suppose. Look, it's getting awfully hot in this, can we get on with it?
Lawrence: Not before time. *(He quickly reads from his copy of the script.)* Right, Dame Goodbody says "Oh, Ermintrude, I shall miss you so much! Your beautiful eyes; your beautiful teeth and smile; your melodious voice; your beautiful legs; and your beautiful tail" and what I want you to do is to move the appropriate body part at the appropriate time, okay? And then, finally, she asks you to do a simple dance, just forwards two steps, backwards two steps, one step to the side and curtsey. Not exactly rocket science. Right, let's try it. Are you ready?
Alex: Mooo.
Lawrence: Good. "Oh, Ermintrude, I shall miss you so much. Your beautiful eyes *(Ermintrude's eyes flutter)*; your beautiful teeth *(Ermintrude nods head and bares teeth)*; your melodious voice *(Ermintrude moos a few bars of a song, eg. Moon River)*; and your beautiful tail *(nothing happens)*." *(Louder.)* "And your beautiful tail *(nothing)*. Jeffrey, can you wiggle your bum, please?
Jeffrey *(Sticks head out)*: What?!
Lawrence: I need you to wiggle your bum, to make the tail swish. Can you make it go round and round?
Jeffrey: You want me to wiggle my bum? I've got 6 GCEs and a City and Guilds Certificate in Construction and you want me to wiggle my bottom? I didn't think my self-esteem could get any lower!

Lawrence: Okay, skip that for now, the rest seems to work all right. Now, we need to try a little dance. Two steps forwards, two back, one to the side and curtsey. *(To Sound.)* Any chance of some dance music?

Sound *(With heavy sarcasm)*: Anything in particular? A bit of garage; hip hop; Charleston; country and western; twist; waltz; salsa; ballroom; flamenco? Could you try and be a teensy bit more specific?

Lawrence *(Under his breath)*: I suppose if you pay peanuts, you get monkeys ... Helpful, as usual, thank you.

Sound: What about this?
> *Plays music from Sugar Plum Fairy - "Everyone's A Fruit and Nutcase".*

Lawrence *(About to complain, but changes his mind)*: Oh, that's actually quite good! I'm so shocked, I don't know what to say.

Sound: You could try thank you, but *properly* this time.

Lawrence *(Under breath)*: You'll want paying next! *(Shouts.)* Just play the tune, will you?

Sound: Always happy to oblige.
> *Plays tune.*

Lawrence: Okay, forwards two.

Alex: Move left and left.

Jeffrey: Hang on, that's right and right, right?

Alex: Yes, that's right, left, left.

Jeffrey: Right, left, left?

Alex: No, just left, left.

Jeffrey: Well, why did you say right first?

Alex *(Exasperatedly)*: I was just agreeing with you!

Jeffrey: Oh.

Lawrence *(Head in hands, whimpering)*: Try again. Please try, just for me, it's not a lot to ask.

Sound *(Sound of tape rewinding, or needle being scratched across disc)*: I've only got one pair of hands, you know!

*Plays music. During this next sequence, **Jeffrey** and **Alex** get out of sync. Fall over each other and begin fighting inside the costume.*

Lawrence: Forwards, two, backwards two, one to the side and curtsey.

Alex (*Simultaneously with Lawrence*): Move left, right, back right, left, side left, left ... What the blazes? ... Get off me, what do you think you are doing?

Fight ensues, ending up with the two halves separated.

Jeffrey: You set me off on the wrong foot! And anyway, how do I know how a sodding cow curtsies?

Alex: Can't you use your imagination!!

Jeffrey: I'm sure you tripped me up on purpose.

*By this time, **Lawrence** is trying to keep them apart, using his clipboard. A bizarre scene with two halves of the cow trying to hit each other, **Lawrence** in the middle, as **Poppy** and **Jasmine** weave back on, clearly having been drinking, carrying a wine bottle each.*

Jasmine: Well, hello! Is this a private party, or can anyone join in?

Poppy (*Takes out phone*): I must have a photo of this! It'll look great on YouTube!

Jeffrey: I don't want my picture taking, not in this outfit, it won't do anything for my image. *(To **Lawrence**.)* It's all your fault. If you were in control of things, none of this would ever have happened!

Poppy (*Loudly*): talking of pictures, have a look at these - you can see what Rupert gets up to! He likes dressing up, don't you, Rupert? Rupert, where are you, I can't see you. Strange ... I can't find my pictures, something's wrong with my phone!

***Rupert** enters.*

Rupert: Keep your voice down, will you? You've been drinking.

Poppy: Oh, *well* spotted! Yes, Jazza and me, we've been partying.

Rupert: *Jazza?*

Poppy: Oh, yes, my new friend. And you know that little problem you kept having, you know, the one which you said would be all right if I kissed it better? Seems that was the reason why Jazza dumped you all those years ago. Like me, she got fed up of you not *standing* up for yourself.

Rupert: You bitch! Ganging up on me now, are you?

Jasmine: Oh, don't be too hard on her, Rupert, you bring it all on yourself! You want the best of all worlds, without any commitment. You're just so shallow, running back to Mandy-moneybags whenever the C-word is mentioned.

Poppy's mobile phone rings.

Poppy *(Looking at phone, puzzled)***:** Funny, I don't recognise that number.

Jasmine: Put it on hands free so we can all have a listen!

Phone plays through sound system.

Voice *(Sharply)***:** Hello? ... Hello, Rupert? ... Are you there? ... Where are you? I need you here at home, I'm going out and the cat needs taking to the vet.

Poppy *(Still tipsy)***:** Hello, who is this?

Voice: Amanda, Amanda Goldsmith, who are you? ... Why are you using my husband's phone? ... Where is he, I want to speak to him!

Poppy: Oh, Mandy, so glad to talk to you at long last! We've got so much to talk about ... sooo much in common.

Rupert: Oh, God! Give me that phone!

Rupert tries to snatch phone off Poppy, who throws phone to Jasmine - Poppy shields Jasmine, Rupert has a sulk.

Voice: Rupert? Who is that woman? What does she mean we have so much in common?

Jasmine: Hello, Amanda,. Poppy and I were just saying how inadequate Rupert is, don't you find?

Throws phone back to Poppy, Jasmine shields.

Voice: Poppy! Isn't she that little tart who works in the theatre?

Poppy: Hello, Amanda, this is the tart speaking. Rupert and I did have a bit of a thing going, but I've finished with him now, you can have him back!

Rupert: Nooooooo!

Jeffrey: Oooh, nasty one that! A bit below the belt.

Alex: You're not kidding! Time to make a retreat, I think - drink?

Jeffrey: You're on. This place gets more like a zoo every day.

Alex and Jeffrey exit "Forwards left, forwards right" etc.

Voice: Rupert - is this true, you bastard? Who else is there with you?

Rupert: Amanda ... Oh, that's just the cow leaving.

Voice: *What?!*

Rupert: No, that doesn't sound right ... Look, I can explain everything.

Voice: Don't bother to even try, Rupert. I've had enough of you. Don't bother coming home - I'm going to have the locks changed. You can go back to the tart - *if* she'll have you!

Poppy: Hello, tart here again, actually, I don't want him either.

Jasmine: And *I* don't want him either.

Voice: Rupert, who is *that*?

Jasmine: Call me Tart Two if you like! No! I know, call me Arty Tart!

Poppy: And you can call me Pop Tart!

Voice: Oh, how amusing! Daddy was considering putting some money into your next production, even though he doesn't think much of Rupert as a husband, but you can forget that now. Rupert, you can contact me through Daddy's solicitor. Drop the car keys through the letter box. I'll put a suitcase of clothes on the front porch. *(Hanging up.)* Goodbye, Rupert.

Rupert: Amanda! ... Wait I can explain. Oh, God! *(Turns on Jasmine and Poppy.)* Well, are you two satisfied now? How the hell did she get to be speaking to you, anyway?

Poppy: Ah, I think you muddled up the SIM cards. You put your card in my phone.

Rupert: What? It was you who showed me the SIM card thing! You did that on purpose, didn't you? You're vindictive and twisted. You couldn't just let it go, could you? You had to ruin everything.

Poppy: There wasn't much left to ruin really, if I remember!

Rupert: I've got nowhere to stay tonight. Where can I go?
Rupert faces up to Poppy in a threatening manner, but is restrained by Jasmine.

Jasmine: Shall I tell him or will you?

Poppy: Don't you dare threaten me, Rupert!
Poppy pushes Rupert, who stumbles backwards into Jasmine who, in fending him off, accidentally hits him, catching his head with her nails.

Rupert: You hit me!

Jasmine: Don't be so pathetic, Rupert, I hardly touched you.

Rupert: I don't believe it, you actually hit me! You're both against me. What is it with women? What have I ever done to deserve any of this? *(Holds hand up to head.)* Blood, there's blood! You've actually wounded me! I can't *(he starts to faint)* ... Ooooh *(he crumples)* ...

Poppy *(To Jasmine)*: Catch him, quick!
They catch Rupert and start to take him off stage.

Jasmine: Typical. Haemophobic! We had better get him to the first-aid room before he does himself any real damage. And they call women the weaker sex!
They exit, carrying Rupert. Lawrence is clearly not coping with any of this.

Sound: This is all very entertaining, but we can't find it in the script - we're a bit lost. Lawrence, Lawrence?

Bea *(Off)*: Lawrence. *(She rushes on, sharply.)* Lawrence! There's a problem with the costumes for the geisha girls dance costumes - they've only gone and sent ballet dresses and I ... Lawrence? ... Lawrence? ... Lawrence?

Lawrence *(Moving to centre spot, starting to break down, becoming more manic as speech progresses)*: I've had as much as I can take, I'm on medication as it is - I'm not very well. All I want to do is to direct a little pantomime, so that kids can come with their Mums and Dads and their Uncles and their Grannies and have a good time: "Look out, he's behind you"; "Oh, no, he isn't"; "Oh, yes, he is." It's not too much to ask, is it? *(Sits, takes piece of blanket out of inside pocket.)* I'm not a bad person, am I? I've not been a bad boy, have I Mummy? Don't do that, Mummy, I'll be a good boy ... I really will try. When's Daddy coming home? Soon? I didn't mean to say that to Uncle Jim, really I didn't. The cat will get better, won't he? Sorry about the wet bed ... Sorry, so sorry. I need my Yummer. *(Starts stroking Yummer, singing softly to himself, rocking backwards and forwards.)* "Daddy wouldn't buy me a Bow Wow ..."

Music - "They're Going To Take Me Away" - gets louder during this speech, as lights fade to a spot on **Lawrence**.

Curtain

Act II, Scene One

The next day

*The curtains open, with a ghost town sound FX, to find **Bea**, **Poppy**, **Jasmine**, **Jeffrey** and **Alex** sitting on the set, looking very morose. The lighting is muted. **Bea** is reading an e-mail; **Alex** is sitting scanning his contract, **Jeffrey** reading a paper and **Jasmine** is doing her nails. The **Cleaning Lady** wanders in, casually dusts a few things, including the beanstalk, and wanders off again. **Alex** moves to downstage centre. Spotlight on **Alex**, rest of lights dim, rest of cast freeze.*

Alex: Being in the spotlight might look glamorous, but it's not, you know. I'm glad that I'm backstage crew - it's only slightly less manic, but without the lipstick and the wigs. If you could see backstage - it's a jumble of wires, bits of wood and string and conflicting egos. Some actors panicking, having a last minute look at their words, others standing quietly in the wings, probably on medication, waiting for their cue to go on. When the actors come off, they are on an adrenaline high, so you have to treat them like a piece of fragile pottery - one slip and they fall to pieces! And as for the Directors! Even worse than the actors. They disagree with Galileo because they think the Earth revolves around them! Look at Lawrence, the only time he didn't want to be the centre of attention was at a funeral. He's not in today - stress apparently. You might think that this *(indicates)* is all over now, but perhaps you ought to stay on to the bitter end, if only out of morbid curiosity!

All unfreeze; light back to muted, spot fades.

Bea *(Blowing nose, she clearly has caught a cold)*: So, that's it then. It's official. We're all washed up and the bank is closing us down - selling off all of the assets. They say that with Lawrence being "incapacitated", they don't think it's appropriate to appoint another director at such a late stage in the production. They can pay us to the end of next week and then - goodbye. Not even "thanks for all you've done"! That's bankers for you - no heart and just red ink for blood.

Alex *(Moving to Bea)*: It says here in my contract that I'm entitled to four weeks' notice.

Bea: It says a lot of things, but they aren't going to happen. Anyway, it's not all about you. What about Lawrence? "Under sedation and must have nothing but rest and quiet." What about the theatre? They can't book any other show in at such short notice, surely?

Jasmine: I heard on the grapevine that the *Teletubbies' Christmas Show* was looking for a venue in the area. Apparently, the theatre they were booked in to was condemned - they'd had a flea circus in the week before and half of the little beggars escaped and started breeding in the stalls.

Bea: That's far more common than you might imagine!

Alex: What, breeding in the stalls?

Bea: No, an infestation of fleas in theatres!

Bea picks up stool and sits behind group. Jeffrey and Jasmine look at each other, then at the audience, and start scratching.

Alex: Surely, we can't just leave it like that? There must be something we can do?

Jeffrey: Like what? No-one has seen Rupert since yesterday; we still haven't replaced Brian and Derek to operate

Ermintrude. Denise, who was playing Jack, has gone for a job at the garden centre. She seems to think that working with the magic beans might give her an edge there. And we are director-less. Oh, and on top of that, the last rehearsal was such a shambles that I don't think anyone in their right mind would want to see it, let alone have to pay money for the privilege.

Poppy: I must admit, I do feel a bit bad about it all. Lawrence has been under a terrific strain trying to put this panto on and I even feel a bit sorry for Rupert. I hope he found somewhere to sleep. He came round to my place at two in the morning, but I wouldn't let him in.

Alex *(Picks up small stepladder, sits behind the others, next to Bea)*: He probably slept in that fancy car of his - he should make use of it while he can. It didn't sound as if he was going to have that for much longer either.

Jasmine: Has the box office started refunding the advance bookings yet?

Bea: I don't think so. There's a big meeting going on with all of the finance people and the theatre manager.

Jasmine: Just who have they sent in to mastermind the closedown, does anyone know?

General shaking of heads.

Alex: I was there when his car arrived. I think he introduced himself as "Brian, Brian Hardmann; Hardmann - with two Ns", I think he said.

Jasmine: Oh, no, no, no! No, no, it couldn't be! I wonder ... No!

Jeffery: Don't tell me, another of your conquests?

Jasmine: Well, I did once have an affair with a Brian Hardmann - with two Ns - and he was a banker. *(To **Alex**.)* Alex, did he have big, bushy eyebrows, have a northern accent and walk with a slight limp? And asthma - he wheezes a lot. Well, he did with me anyway.

Alex: I did notice that he had a bit of an accent and it did sound a bit "'ee bah gum"-ish. He said he "wanted nowt" when he was offered a drink. And he used a posh cane while walking, it had a silver top to it. Now that you come to mention it, I think I saw him use an inhaler as well.

Jasmine: That must be him. How very interesting!

Bea: He doesn't sound your type at all: an asthmatic, northern banker with a limp? Far too conventional and boring.

Jasmine: Actually, darling, it was just the opposite! It was the things he got up to at the weekends that make him stand out in my mind! You wouldn't believe it - he liked wearing my clothes, for a start. He adored fish-net stockings. Oh, yes and then there was that business with the floor polisher ...

Alex: A floor polisher? ... The mind positively boggles.

Jasmine: Let's not go there just at the moment. No *(pauses and smiles)* ... No, but the point is, I might have a little bit of leverage over him, if you know what I mean.

Jeffery: I doubt that you could get him to change his mind about closing us down - there's far too much money at stake.

Jasmine: No, but I might just be able to persuade him to come and see the show and perhaps give us a bit of an extension before a final decision is made.

Bea: Just one slight problem - we don't have a show for him to see at the moment, remember?

Poppy: We don't even know where Rupert is. We can't put on a panto without the Baron: he's one of the principal characters.

Alex: Oh, yes, we can! *(All look at him askance.)* Sorry, couldn't resist it! I could have a go at doing something - just a small part. I've always fancied myself as a bit of an actor, just never had the nerve to do it.

Bea: I heard you practicing on stage when you thought no-one was looking, you were really good.

Alex: Oh, now that's embarrassing! I must have sounded like a right idiot.

Bea: Not at all, you are a real natural, but why were you reciting Juliette's balcony speech? Have you ever done any acting?

Alex: Only at primary school - I was the third sheep in the nativity play. I only had to say "Baaaah" to the Angel Gabriel and "Baaaah Baaaah" to the baby Jesus. But I did rise to the dizzy heights of playing Juliet in *Romeo and Juliet* at secondary school - it was an all-boys school - that explains what I was doing when you heard me. Someone had to dress up as a girl, but no-one wanted to do it. The teacher had either me or a boy called Trevor in mind for the part. Trevor was the class bully and so I had my arm twisted, literally, until I agreed to do it. I got a lot of stick when I had to wear a dress and stuff a pair of socks inside my t-shirt, but once I started to perform in front of an audience, I actually quite enjoyed it. I was able to pick up words really quickly, that helped a lot.

Jasmine: Look, I know that I've been against doing a pantomime right from the start, but I need this job at the moment - my inheritance is all in shares and have you seen the state of the stock market? So, if I can manage to buy us a bit of time from Brian, could you have a go at taking the part of Jack, just for a scene or two?

Alex: Oh, I didn't mean anything as big as that! I don't think I could learn the words that quickly.

Jeffrey: I don't want to have to keep looking for jobs either. I tell you what - we could help you out with the words. I've got an idea that might just work. *(To Jasmine.)* Do you think we could get away with doing just a couple of scenes for Hardmann, with his two Ns?

Jasmine: I don't know, he's probably a busy man, so we might just get away with that. He probably won't want to hang around me for too long anyway. *(To **Alex**.)* Go on, Alex, give it a go - what have we got to lose? You never know, it might even be fun.

Alex: Okay, I'll give it a go, but what about Rupert? *(Moves to Poppy.)* Poppy, you've got to try and get him back somehow.

Poppy: I suppose I could try ringing him. Doing something positive might take his mind off things for a bit. And he's going to need every penny he can lay his hands on, now that Amanda has given him the heave-ho.

Jasmine: In that case, I'll go and meet with Hardmann and try to see if I can get him to agree to see us and perhaps arrange a time. Alex, you go and try the costume on and Poppy, see what you can do about Rupert. Can we meet back here at say 2 o'clock? *(All agree.)* Jeffrey, can you sort out the stage? Okay, just one more thing *(goes to wings, brings on floor polisher)* I think this might come in handy! Here I come, Brian, ready or not!

Jasmine switches on floor polisher and exits.

Poppy *(Gets up to go)*: I'm not at all sure about this. If Jasmine comes on too strong, it might not do Hardmann any good at all, with everything that's wrong with him, she might polish him off!

Jeffrey *(Exiting)*: Now, that's exactly what I thought she had in mind ...!

Curtain

Scene Two

A little later

*Curtains open on **Jeffrey** standing looking useless, **Bea** is busy putting props in appropriate places. **Alex** enters.*

Jeffrey: I'm worn out, I need a sit down. *(Sits.)* How did the costume fitting go?

Alex *(Sits)*: Not bad, Bea had to take it in a bit around the waist, but it should be okay. I've had a go at some of the words as well, but there's far too many to learn in just a day. What was it you had in mind to help me with them?

Jeffrey: You'll see. I've got it covered, don't you worry. *(Takes out mobile phone.)* Hey, I had a text this morning about a job I'm interested in, B&Q - small tools section. Just up my street.

Alex: You won't have far to drive then? *(No reaction.)* Just up your street? ... Get it?

Jeffrey *(With irony)*: You should be on the stage! Oh, you already are. They want me to send in my CV. What is a CV anyway?

Bea *(Turns to join in conversation)*: I remember doing about those at school, in PSHE. About the only useful thing I can remember doing in PSHE.

Jeffrey: CV - PSHE - me no speaky the lingo!

Alex: A CV is generally a sheet of waffle and exaggeration about what you've got in the way of qualifications and what work you've done in the past.

Jeffrey: So what exactly does it stand for?

Alex: Curriculum Vitae - CV.

Jeffrey: But that's not even English! So when did you do your CVs, then?

Alex: In our PHSE lessons. Sometimes we were actually allowed to go in to the computer suite and touch the computers for a change, rather than write about stuff.

Bea (Sits): A lot of the lads mucked about at my school, trying to download games and mucky pictures. The teacher was forever trying to ban them from the internet.

Alex: Everyone did that! But I did actually produce a CV. I used it when I went for my college interview. It had on it which schools I had been to, what GCSEs I had got and what my interests were.

Jeffery: But you said that CVs are all waffle and exaggeration.

Bea: Well, people make things sound much grander than they really are.

Jeffery: Such as?

Alex: Well, say you had a part-time job for a pizza company and you often delivered pizzas to the actors at a theatre, you could put "regular theatregoer" or "experience of theatrical catering" or "personal assistant to ..." - just add in the name of anyone you served a pizza to. They're all sort of true, but they are not things people can check up on.

Jeffrey: What about actual qualifications?

Bea: Well, they can be checked up on, of course. But checking it all costs time and money, so as long as you are careful, you can get away with a lot.

Jeffrey: Can you help me with mine then, for this job?

Alex: No worries. Bea, can we use your laptop to mock something up?

Bea: Yes, of course, I'll just go and fetch it.

Bea exits.

Jeffrey: I wasn't expecting to have to start applying for jobs again. I thought that this job would go on for years yet.

Alex: I'm not sure what I'm going to do, but I love the entertainment business. Even working here has been okay until now. I might apply for a job on a cruise ship or something, get out and see a bit of the world. Let's face it, almost any job would be an improvement on what it's like here, the way things are going at the moment.

Bea *(Enters with laptop)*: Here we are. *(Opens laptop and starts typing.)* Right, Curriculum Vitae for Jeffrey - Jeffrey Staines, isn't it? What's your date of birth?

Alex: I know he's Taurus - he's always checking his horoscope.

Bea: Oh, I believe in all of that, it's scary how often it comes true. I'm a Virgo, you know. Only the other day, my horoscope said "some money might be coming your way" and, would you believe it, that same day, some nice Nigerian gentleman e-mailed me saying he needed some help getting his money out of the country and, if I sent him my bank details to put the money in, he would share it with me.

Alex: You didn't, *did* you??

Bea: Well, it does sound an easy way to boost my bank balance.

Jeffery: We were told something about that on a course I went on: "Safe Use of Computers in the Workplace". It's called Phishing, isn't it?

Bea: Fishing? What do you mean? My Dad used to go fishing. I went with him once or twice. It usually meant him sleeping by the side of the river all day and drowning maggots. I think it was just an excuse to get away from my Mum for a bit. But what's that got to do with computer fishing?

Alex: No, they go phishing for your bank details. It's spelt P.H.I.S.H.I.N.G. As soon as you give them your bank details, you'll certainly see a change in your bank balance, but not the sort of change you were hoping for.

Bea: I think I'll give that a miss then. Good job I'm due a tax rebate from the Inland Revenue. £2,000 the e-mail said, but they just needed to confirm my bank ... Oh, no, you don't think, do you? It looked really official.

Alex: You haven't sent your details have you?

Bea: No, not yet, I only got it the other day and I haven't had time to reply. *(Takes paper from laptop bag.)* I've got a printout here.

Alex: Weren't you at all suspicious?

Bea: I did think £2,000 was a lot to get back. (Shows Alex the e-mail.) Look, here it is.

Alex: The heading looks authentic enough, let's have a look. *(Reading from paper, with emphasis on the misspelled words.)* "Dearest *Sirs* or *Madams*, Please be *accepting* the news that you are *entitling* to refund of $2,000" - dollars! - "This has *eventualised* as a result of a *taxing* overpayment. Please to advise us of your bank *accounting* details by e-mail for the *transferrings* of the money, which will be credited on receipt of. *Regardings* at this time, I. M. Hacker." You must be joking!

Bea: I did think the English was a bit dodgy, but I just thought that perhaps they were using someone on work experience from the local comprehensive to do the letters. I just needed the money so badly, I wanted it to be true.

Alex: That's the really sad thing, they con money out of the people who can least afford it.

Jeffrey: I've had some really strange women contact me on one of those computer dating websites. Some of them were after me doing some very novel things. One of them said that as I worked in the theatre, could she perform on stage with me? And I don't think she meant Shakespeare. She wasn't the worst and I'm not sure that some of them were even women, you know.

Alex: You can't be too careful with the internet, there's some dodgy people out there.

Bea: This isn't getting this CV done, you know. I haven't got all day and Jasmine should be back soon. What date of birth are you?

Jeffrey: May 1st 1965.

Bea types in his responses.

Bea: Secondary School?
Jeffrey: Leicester City Boys.
Alex: Approved was it?
Jeffrey glares at him.
Bea: O-level passes?
Jeffrey: English, Maths, Geography, Science and Technology
Alex: You said that you had got 6 O-levels - that's only 5!
Jeffrey: Science counted as two for some reason, it's all to do with being -ologies, I think.
Bea: That sounds a bit dodgy. What about the grades?
Alex: Just put them down as passes - too much information can be counter-productive.
Bea: Oh, I see, not so good then? Okay, passes it is. Did you do A-levels?
Jeffrey: No, I left at 16 and went to the local Poly and did my City and Guilds in Construction.
Alex: So you didn't read Classics at Cambridge then?
Jeffrey *(Glares again and stands up)*: No, but it's funny you should say that - the Poly turned into a University just after I left! *(Points at computer screen.)* So put down "Construction Technology" at the University of the East Midlands - sounds proper good that!
Bea: Have you got any other certificates?
Jeffrey: Cycling Proficiency any good? Bronze Swimming 100 metres?
Bea: Not really, what about interests?
Alex: Well he spends most of his day lounging around here looking at the newspaper, so put down "active theatre-goer, reads a lot".
Bea *(Doubtfully)*: Ye-s. Last bit of the CV for now then, Employment History.
Jeffrey *(Wandering)*: I had a paper-round when I was 11 - flipping heavy those papers were, especially with all of the Sunday Supplements - bent the saddlebag on my

bike! I remember complaining about it at the time. And then I washed cars for extra pocket money, but the detergent played havoc with the skin on my hands and my Mum wouldn't let me use her rubber gloves, so I had to give that up and then when I was 14, I ...

Alex: Stop! Stop, for goodness sake! We don't need to go back as far as the introduction of child labour laws or the abolition of the slave trade! I'm beginning to see how you've become such a lazy, cantankerous old sod!

Jeffrey: Sarcasm is the lowest form of wit. You said to put down everything relevant and my formative years gave me a wealth of experience in the ways that employers exploit their workers. Someone has to speak up on behalf of the oppressed and make their lives just a little happier, just a little safer.

Bea: I can't make up my mind who you most remind me of - Mother Theresa or Stalin!

Alex: Just put down any proper paid jobs as an adult. We don't need to know how you earned an extra Saturday sixpence by tidying up your bedroom.

Jeffrey (*Moving around, thoughtfully*)**:** After College I worked for BT. Poles 'n' 'Oles section. But I got involved with the union, they sent me on all these Health and Safety courses, so, what with meetings, safety inspections and strikes, I managed to get away with not doing very much. I got redundancy a year or two after they privatised - 1984 that was - got quite a decent package considering I hadn't worked there all that long.

Bea: So where's all that gone, then? Wine, women and gambling and you wasted the rest?

Jeffrey: Huh, I wish! No, I spent most of it on the house (*bitterly*) ... which the ex has now got. Then I had a few bits and pieces of work, but not much permanent, until I ended up here.

Alex: Don't forget the undertakers!

Jeffrey: Oh, yes, I didn't last long there. We had a falling out. After I dropped one of their customers, they dropped me sharpish! *(Moves to Bea, points at screen.)* Put "1990-1991, Funeral Industry".

Bea: Reason for leaving?

Alex: Put down "I wanted my career to go in a different direction from my employers" - that just about covers it.

Bea: I'll go to the office and tidy this up a bit, see if I can get a printed copy done. See you later.

Alex helps Bea with the laptop and papers. Bea exits.

Jeffrey: I've learned a lot this morning. Think I need a bit of a sit down - fancy a cuppa?

Alex: Yes, I do!

Jeffrey *(Sits)***:** While you're up, you can make me one as well. Ta.

Alex: You don't change, do you? Okay, I'll make it. *(Goes to kettle upstage. Shouts.)* She's really nice is Bea.

Jeffrey: I thought you had taken a bit of a shine to her. Why don't you ask her out?

Alex: I think I would have done before all of this closing down business, but everything's too uncertain at the moment - I don't know where either of us will be working or living. If I can't afford my rent, I might even have to move back home to my parents in Doncaster for a while. Doncaster - God forbid! *(Brings 2 mugs with tea bags in and a bottle of milk to table.)* Anyway, here's your tea, I should leave it to mash a bit before you take the bag out.

Poppy and Jasmine enter, with floor polisher.

Jasmine: Well, I managed to buy us a bit of time. It was touch and go for a while, but when I started mentioning giving him a good buffing, he went a bit red in the face, muttered a bit and relented. He said that if we can convince him that we have a show, he will try to persuade the bank that we are viable for a bit longer. Any luck with Rupi, Poppy?

Poppy *(Stands to inspect polisher)*: I eventually managed to get hold of him. Apparently, he is camped out in their old summerhouse. I persuaded him to come in later this afternoon. I had to explain to him how to catch a bus, for God's sake! His car was towed away this morning and the hole in the wall machine ate his card, so he's got no money for a taxi and he didn't know how to get here - poor thing!

Jasmine: Talk about "how are the mighty fallen"! Even I'm feeling a bit sorry for him. No, on second thoughts, I'm not - he brought it all on himself. Now, Brian will be in the auditorium early this evening, so who have we got and which scene shall we do for him?

Alex *(Stands to inspect polisher)*: I've tried to learn the scenes where I give Ermintrude to the strange old woman on the way to the fair, and she gives me a bag of beans, which I take home to you, mumsie.

Jasmine: Don't push your luck, sunshine! Yes, that sounds about right. We need the Dame, that's me. The Baron, hopefully Rupert. Jack, that's you, Alex. The old woman dressed in rags, anyone can do that, she only has a couple of lines. We'll drag one of the cleaners in, she won't even have to change. That just leaves Ermintrude - Jeffrey?

Jeffrey *(Removes teabags, adds milk)*: I knew that was coming.

Jasmine: Well, believe it or not, it looks like we can't do this without you, so what do you say?

Jeffrey *(Sipping tea, thoughtfully)*: I can't do it.

Jasmine *(Moving behind Jeffrey)*: What? After all the effort everyone else has made? Why on Earth can't you do it? I know you haven't got much time for actors and, by the way, the feeling is rather mutual, but even you must have a heart somewhere.

Jeffrey *(Smugly)*: Because, my dear Jasmine, it takes two to tango! I can't do it on my own, even if I wanted to. I need someone else in the costume with me.

Poppy: Yes, of course. I thought it was all going too well. Any ideas anyone? *(Singing heard in the background.)* At least someone sounds happy. That's not Lawrence, is it?

Alex *(Looking off)***:** It is, but it isn't.

Jasmine: Well, that's clear, then! What do you mean "it is, but it isn't"?

Alex: Well, it's his head, but the body looks wrong somehow ...

Jasmine: What!? What are you talking about?

Alex: You'll see for yourself in a moment.

Lawrence enters, slowly, as if in a dream, hair awry, but with a big fixed grin, clutching a bottle of pills.

Lawrence *(As if drugged)***:** I've got some lovely medicine which the kind doctor gave me. She said I needed cheering up because I have been under a lot of stress. These little yellow pills make me feel all warm and fuzzy inside, like a little furry kitten. Meow.

Jeffrey *(Putting tea down)***:** Oh my God, what have they given him?

Alex: It looks like he is on "Happy" pills. How many have you taken, Lawrence? ... Lawrence? *(As if talking to an idiot, Lawrence not really comprehending.)* Do try to concentrate. Look, we need you to do a bit of acting. We are going to do a bit of the pantomime. There is someone important in the audience who might be able to help save the company, but we need to convince him that we can do the pantomime. We are going to do the part where Jack takes Ermintrude to be sold and we need you to take part.

Lawrence: I'm the director. *(Giggles.)* He-he-he. You all have to do what I say. Let's all play at being little furry animals.

Jasmine *(Moving to Lawrence)***:** That's a great idea, Lawrence, you can play at being a nice little cow.

Lawrence: I like moo cows. Moo - moo.

Jasmine: That's perfect. Jeffrey, if you go at the back, then perhaps you can steer him

Alex: Steer him - I like that one!
Jasmine *(With a withering look)*: Shut up, Alex! We haven't got time for your daft jokes.
Jeffrey *(Stands)*: No, we haven't. Now, about helping you out with your words, if you get stuck, just say "worms" to Poppy and then she will know that you need a cue.
Alex: What? Worms?
Jeffrey: Yes, work it into the conversation as naturally as you can.
Alex: How can you work worms into a conversation??
Lawrence *(Sings)*: "There's a worm at the bottom of my garden, and his name is Wiggly-woo."
Poppy: I'm worried about him.
Jeffrey: We're stuck with him. I'll do my best with him at the front of Ermintrude, but I can't promise.
Alex: You could try *bull*-ying him! *(Jeffrey and Jasmine give him a hard stare.)* Sorry.
Jeffrey: Just remember, if you can't remember your words, just say worms.
Alex: Worms. Got it ...I think.
Jeffrey and Alex exit muttering.
Jasmine: This is our last chance, then. We've got a stagehand in the leading role; an incompetent bigot and a psycho inside a cow costume. We don't know if the Baron can afford the bus fare to get here ...
Poppy *(Exiting, turns to audience)*: And a posh bint out of her comfort zone as the Dame! Sounds like the perfect pantomime.

Curtain

Sound effect of a train crash.
Sound: Sorry.

Optional Troubadour

Front of curtain, during scene change. To the tune of "Greensleeves".

Troubadour: They sent me out here to sing you a song,
The Stage Manager said that they won't be long.
So here I stand to tell you this tale,
Of a pantomime that was doomed to fail.

Jeffrey is idle but Alex is cool,
Rupert gets used to playing the fool.
Lawrence gets crazy and Bea gets mad,
Jasmine gets drunk and poor Poppy is sad.

Alex sold their cow for some magic beans,
But all he's got left are shattered dreams.
His Mum's dead mad that he sold Ermintrude,
'Cos they haven't any money for rent, nor food.
A Posh bint out of her comfort zone,
The leading man thrown out of his home.
All the ingredients of a major disaster,
Will make the ending come much faster.

Will fairy magic redeem the day,
And will Jack the role of the hero play?
With magic beans dashed to the ground,
It will all end in ruin, I'll be bound!

Scene Three

The Panto scene

There is plenty of scope here for a dance scene, eg with The Forest Sprites - probably not very young children in light of the other material in the play, but could even be adults dressed up as Sprites. Alternatively, a dream sequence dance could be set.

On the way to the fair - a dark area, with trees, a stump to sit on, with a storm approaching in the distance. To "Teddy Bear's Picnic", enter **Alex** *as Jack, carrying a red-spotted handkerchief on a stick, and* **Ermintrude**, *whose front end is a little unsteady - "Left a bit, stop, no, not there" etc all heard from inside* **Ermintrude**.

Alex: Poor old thing, it seems such a shame to have to sell you after all these years, but we haven't any money to pay the Baron for his rent, and we can't afford to feed you anymore. Oh, Ermintrude, I'm so sorry. If only I had tried harder to get a job, like Mother wanted. But I will try really hard to find you a nice rich master who will look after you and give you a nice clean warm shed with plenty of .. plenty of ... worms ... worms!?
Alex looks in a panic at Poppy in the wings.
Lawrence: Moo?
Jeffrey *(Sticks head out of costume)*: She's lost her voice!
Alex: What?
Jeffrey: She's lost her voice - she caught a cold off Bea!
Alex: How on Earth is she going to prompt me?! What about my worms?
Jeffrey: Pictures. She's going to use pictures. Look, use your imagination.
Poppy *(Holds up a picture of a sweet, a nose and a haystack)*: Here.

Alex: Yes, not worms, no, that would be silly, wouldn't it, no some ... sweet ... smelling ... hay to eat. You don't mind, do you?

Lawrence: Meow, meow.

Scuffle inside costume.

Jeffrey: No, Lawrence, let *me* do the talking. Moo.

Lawrence: Meow.

Jeffrey: Shut up!

Alex: There's still a long way to go and I'm getting tired. Here, let's have a sit down for a few minutes. *(Sits on a log, Ermintrude looks around, then back and tries to sit on his knee.)* I'm ever so thirsty, I could really do with a drink to keep me going.

Rubs his hands, takes a small bucket out of his pack and makes as if to milk Ermintrude, who reacts, puts up hoof to stop him.

Jeffrey: Whoa there!

Sound FX gurgling etc. Ermintrude crosses legs etc. Carton of milk appears from flap in udders.

Alex: Wow, that's impressive, how did you do that?

A howling wind blows leaves onto the stage - a bit scary with scary sounds. Lightning crashes, lighting up eyes in the branches of the trees.

Alex: I don't like the look of this, Ermintrude, its dark and scary and my knees are starting to shake.

Jeffrey: Moooo!

Ermintrude's knees start to shake - sound effect initially wrong. Alex looks askance at the sound team.

Sound: Oops!

Crash of lightning, Ermintrude shakes even more, then produces a carton of pink milk-shake.

Alex: If I'd known you could do that, we could have set up a business. Mind you, it's really expensive setting up a business - what would we have used for *cow*-lateral?

Groans from offstage.

Jeffrey: Moooo!

Alex: I've got a good idea. Whenever I feel afraid I find that whistling helps me to stay calm. *(Whistles "Whenever I Feel Afraid".)* Are you any good at whistling, Ermintrude?

Lawrence: Meow.

Jeffrey: For Pete's sake, Lawrence, shut up and let me do the mooing.

Alex *(Kicks Ermintrude, causing a kerfuffle)*: Perhaps the people out there can help us?

*Ermintrude does a double-take, seeing the audience for the first time, puts giant glasses on from **Bea**. Optional Audience participation.*

Alex *(To audience)*: Will you help us whistle?

Audience whistle.

Alex *(To audience)*: Well, that was rubbish! Anyhow, I feel so much braver now, but all this exercise has made me even more tired. Perhaps I could just rest for a little while, as I'm so sleepy. *(Yawns and lies down in a corner.)* You can stand guard, Ermintrude, and let me know if anyone comes.

Ermintrude *nods, stands to attention and erratically marches up and down, until Jack falls asleep. Thunder and lightning.* **Old Woman** *(the cleaning lady) is pushed on to the stage using a mop. She has a basket of sticks, which clearly contain her words. She walks around muttering, picking up sticks.* **Ermintrude** *tries to wake up* **Alex**, *but by the time he is awake, the* **Old Woman** *has gone.*

Alex: What is it Ermintrude? ... I was fast asleep!

Jeffrey: Moooo, mooooo, mooooooooo, moo, mooooooh!

Alex: What's that, Ermintrude? You saw someone? An old woman?

Jeffrey: Moooo.

Alex: But there's no one there, now.

*****Old Woman*** appears behind him.**

Audience: She's behind you.

Alex: Oh, no, she isn't!

Audience: Oh, yes, she is!

Alex: Oh, no, she isn't!

Old Woman *(Looking at words in bundle of sticks)*: I'm sorry if I startled you, but I don't often see people here in the woods. I'm gathering sticks to light a fire: it gets so cold at night and I've not had a hot meal for ages. The Baron has taken what little money I had for rent. Oh, dear.

Alex: I wish there was something I could give you, but I haven't any money, either.

Old Woman: Don't you worry about me, dear, I'll be all right. I just need to gather a few more sticks for my fire. *(Picks up more sticks.)* I'll just have a little rest for a few minutes and then I'll get on my way. *(She staggers and sits on the stump.)* Oh, I'm so tired, I don't know if I can go on much longer.

Alex: I'll help you. *(Tries to gather sticks, but can't find any. Shouts off.)* Sticks, where are the sticks? *(A bundle of sticks, still in polythene, is thrown on.)* Here you are. I wish I had some ... some ... Oh, what was it? Worms! Some worms, I need worms!! *(Looks in panic towards wings.* **Poppy** *draws a bag of gold.)* That's it, I need gold ... er ... that is golden worms ... That's it, I wish I had a bag of golden worms to give you.

Old Woman looks puzzled at **Ermintrude**, who shrugs shoulders.

Old Woman *(Looking in panic at her script)*: You're a good, kind boy, but you don't need to give me your ... golden worms! I'll be all right, I'll get by ... Somehow.

Alex: No, wait. I have got something to give you. You must take Ermintrude. She will be a faithful friend to you and will give you creamy fresh milk when you are hungry.

Old Woman *(Patting Ermintrude)*: Oh, I couldn't take your cow, I have nothing to give you in exchange - only this bag of magic beans.

Alex: Magic beans? They sound like a really good idea. I'm sure Mum would approve of me selling Ermintrude for a ... er ... er *(panics)* ... worms! *(***Ermintrude** *puts hoof over eyes,* **Poppy** *draws a tin of beans.)* No, that's it, beans! Magic beans.

Old Woman: You have such a kind heart. Thank you. *(Takes Ermintrude, puts a scarf around her neck and starts to lead her off, Jeffrey trying to steer Lawrence in the right direction.)* Here are your beans, be careful how you use them. Use them properly and you will be well-rewarded.
Alex is counting his beans and does not notice the Old Woman throwing off her cloak and, with a flash, transforming into Jack's Fairy Godmother - bent wand etc. She waves her wand at Alex who freezes in position and she comes to the front of the stage, with the spot on her.

Old Woman: A selfless deed from a heart that's true,
Deserves all the best to come to you.
As Jack goes home to his Mum, the Dame,
I wish on him riches, health and fame.
*Blackout, flash as **Old Woman** and **Ermintrude** disappear - **Ermintrude** by now splitting into two, **Lawrence** wanders off very unsteadily.*

Alex: Wow, that was a strange dream, the old woman and the chick with the frock, but I must get on to the market to sell Ermintrude. *(Looks around.)* Where is she now? Where has she got to? *(Remembers bag of beans in hand.)* Oh no, it wasn't a dream! I've given Ermintrude away for a bag of beans! What on Earth will Mother say? Oh, I'm for it, now! Oh dear, oh dear. Oh dear!
Alex trudges off, to the accompaniment of sad music - tries whistling, but it doesn't work.

Blackout and final crash of lightning.

Troubadour sings again, during scene change, at front of curtain or audience participation song.

Scene Four

Back at the Cottage

Jasmine *(Looks out of cottage door)*: I can see Jack coming back at last. We are going to be rich! *(Exits cottage, does little dance.)* I can pay off the Baron. Pay off what I owe the catalogue for my new frock and, perhaps, I can have a little holiday, a few days in *(insert name of nearby town)* would be nice. Oh, I'm so excited!
Jasmine sings "Money, Money, Money".
Alex: Hi Mum, I'm back.
Jasmine: Hello, son, lovely to see you etc etc. Let's have it, then - show me all of the lovely lolly, the loot!
Alex: Mum, I've got something better than a bag of gold!
Jasmine *(Incredulous)*: *Better* than a bag of gold? What did you get? Diamonds? Rubies? Prince Harry's phone number? *(Comes over all silly.)* Whoo!
Alex *(After a long silence)*: Beans *(backing away)* ... magic beans, actually!
Jasmine *(Snaps out of reverie)*: Beans!! Beans!! You sold Ermintrude for a bag of worthless beans?!! ... Come here! ... You just wait 'til I get my hands on you, you ... you ...
*Alex starts to run off, but bumps into **Rupert** who has just entered.*
Rupert *(Villainously)*: Watch where you are going, you stupid boy! *(Dusts himself down.)* Now then, Dame Goodbody, where is my rent money? It's pay up *or* pay dearly time. Ooh, I hope it's "pay dearly" time! I love a good eviction!
Rupert mimes throwing them out. Boo's from offstage.
Jasmine: Oo-er! Look, Baron, there's been a *slight* hitch. I sent Jack to sell Ermintrude at the market and he didn't ... er ... He didn't get quite as much as I expected. *(Nervous laugh.)*

Rupert: You can't fool me. I can see that you have a bagful of money there - hand it over.

Jasmine: But, but, but ...

Rupert *(Spitting out words)*: Your pathetic prevarications are only postponing the process. *(Jasmine wipes face with a hanky - pulls hanky from inside bloomers - turns into a string of hankies.)* Tell me, boy, what did you get for the cow?

Alex *(Quickly, garbled)*: Well, it's like this, you see. I went into the woods, but I fell asleep, and Ermintrude gave me a milkshake, but the old woman hadn't got any money so I gave her ... Oh, good grief! Er ... worms ... worms!

Rupert: What? Where? What are you blathering about, boy?

Alex: Worms!

Rupert: You can get ointment for that at the chemist

Alex *(Panicking, goes to Poppy at side of stage)*: Worms?

Poppy *(Rifles through several cards, shakes head, croaks)*: I don't know where you are, make something up.

Alex: What?

Poppy: Tell him about the beans

Alex *(To Rupert, panicking)*: Beans, cow, Old Woman, bag of beans!

Jasmine *(Croaks)*: Tell him that they are magic beans!

Alex: Yes, m-m-magic beans, your Baron-ness.

Rupert: Pah! You are just wasting my time! Give them to me, boy!

Rupert snatches the beans and throws them in the direction of the beanstalk. Flash as Fairy enters, she waves wand and everyone freezes. Her script is attached to wand.

Old Woman: A pound of carrots, some tripe and Vim ... Oh, sorry, that's me shopping list! Oh, dear, where is it, now? ... Ah, here it is ... *(She turns the paper round.)*
It's time for my magic to work its charm,
So that Jack and his Mum come to no harm.
In store for them I have a grand surprise,
As the magic beans grow before their very eyes!

Dramatic sound effect, flash of lights. The beanstalk is supposed to grow at this point, but the "motor" gives up the ghost with the beanstalk at half-mast. Even though frozen, they all look on in horror as it makes an awful noise. Jeffrey (still with back half of cow costume on) sidles in to kick the motor, this causes sparks to fly out of it and shocks his foot, to which he reacts loudly, finding a fire blanket to wrap round his leg and a fire extinguisher - which produces a smoke effect. Lawrence wanders in (clutching a big bottle of pills and still in a daze) and bumps in to the dodgy cottage, which collapses slowly like a pack of cards, the window cleverly passing over Jasmine. Bea rushes in, trips over the edge of the fallen cottage, and falls into Alex's arms. Poppy rushes in to help Jeffrey untangle the beanstalk, which traps them. Old Woman looks at her wand and starts to sidle off.

Old Woman: Ooh, I need to get this wand serviced!
Lights flicker, plus flash effects, then blackout.
Sound: Oops!
Lights slowly come back on to reveal carnage, everyone on stage in disarray. Lawrence clearly traumatised, Poppy clutching on to Rupert, Bea clutching on to Alex. Jeffrey clearly suffering from electric shock, Jasmine's clothes awry etc. Stunned silence. Sound of Jasmine's phone receiving a message: Jasmine reads it out.

Jasmine: Oh, it's a message from Brian. "Funniest thing I've seen in ages. Will recommend a stay of execution. Loved the bit with the cottage falling down and the beanstalk going up in flames - can't wait to see what happens next. Come and see me sometime and we can catch up on old times. Bring Buffy with you!"

Lawrence: Buffy?

Jasmine: Don't ask!

Jeffrey: You've got to be joking! I think that we broke just about every safety code in the book! It's going to take me a week to fill in all of the paperwork. The Inspectorate will be down on us like a ton of bricks. Where are all the Risk Assessments? What if the curtains aren't fire-proof?

Alex *(Holding Bea)*: Are you okay?

Bea: Ummm, I think so, but don't let go, *not* just yet.

Alex grins.
Alex *(Thinking out loud)*: I suppose we could rig up the beanstalk to go up in flames like that, using some sort of stage effect?
Poppy: We can but try. What about you, Rupert?
Rupert: I haven't got anywhere to stay ...
Poppy: I suppose you could sleep on my sofa for a day or two, just until ... you know.
Rupert: Could I? I promise to be good.
Poppy: Just the sofa! Nothing else, mind!
Alex: *Sofa* so good!
All: Oh, Alex!!
*Lights fade to **Alex** in the spotlight, everyone freezes.*
Alex: Of course, it won't really work out. There's no "and they all lived happily ever after", like there is in pantomime - the bankers will see to that. Bea and I are off to work on a cruise ship. I hope we get to bunk up together! That would be nice. Jeff will probably get turned down by B&Q, but then he'll probably go on a course to train to be a traffic warden - his perfect job that. Poppy will probably drift back to Rupert, who will most likely move in with her. She'll get work in a big theatre and move up in the world, while he mopes around the flat, watching daytime TV. Lawrence will move on to directing adverts for cat food; and as for Jasmine, well, she'll get to star in the East Grimsthorpe production of *Aladdin*, alongside someone who came third in the *X-Factor* two years ago - I forget his name. But there's something magical about live theatre, just for a short time, you can make believe that anything is possible, absolutely anything ...
Music - "A Live Show" has slowly been building. Dramatic effects as everyone unfreezes and burst into song, with a little dance routine and curtain calls.

Final Curtain

Properties

Act I, Scene One

On Set
1) Various Props scattered.
2) Paint and paintbrushes.
3) Cottage part assembled.
4) Stepladders (one medium size, one small).
5) Small packing crate, table centre/left stage. Two crates around table, 1 small, battered armchair (**Jeffrey's** chair).
6) One stool.
7) Beanstalk in heap on floor, attached to a pulley.
8) Electric motor, with lots of wires hanging out.

Personal Props
Jeffrey: Bag of chips, newspaper (with horoscope, Lonely Hearts page and crossword)
Alex: Screwdriver
Lawrence: Clipboard with lots of paperwork, man-bag, mobile phone.
Bea: Various bits of costume

Scene Two

On Set
Cottage erected (but wobbly!).

Personal Props
Rupert: Mobile phone (with easily accessible SIM card).
Poppy: Mobile phone (with easily accessible SIM card).

Scene Three

On Set
1) Slightly tidier. Paint and brushes for **Alex** and **Jeffrey**.
2) A small chair, stage left, for **Poppy**.

Personal Props
Bea: A hot-water bottle, blanket and several hot-water bottles on string, tea-cosy for hat. Pantomime cow costume.
Rupert: Squire costume.
Jasmine: Dame costume, a large coloured hankie string. Wine bottle, almost empty.
Poppy: Panto script (in large print), knitting, big box of tissues. Wine bottle, almost empty. Mobile phone.
Lawrence: Clipboard, small piece of comfort blanket.

Act II, Scene One

On Set
1) Small steps for **Alex**.

Personal Props
Alex: Paper headed Contract.
Jeffrey: Newspaper.
Bea: Mobile phone.
Jasmine: Floor polisher.

Scene Two

On Set
1) Small box upstage left, with kettle, milk bottle, tea bags, two mugs.

Personal Props
Jeffrey: Mobile phone.
Bea: Props - twigs, etc. Laptop and laptop bag with papers in.
Lawrence: Large bottle of pills (with *Smarties* in).

Scene Three

On Set
The Scary Forest - we used a painted curtain (scary wood scene) to cover up the cottage.
1) Tree stump downstage right. A few twigs (not many).
2) Leaves, to be blown onto set - fan offstage.
3) Flash effect.
4) Mop (offstage, to push Old Woman on to the set).
5) Small plastic bag bundle of sticks.

Personal Props
Alex: Red, spotted handkerchief on stick. Small backpack with small pail attached.
Poppy: Three pieces of A3 card. Large felt-tip pens.
Jeffrey: Carton of milk, carton of pink milkshake - inside costume.
Old Woman: Basket with a few sticks in. Words, clearly labelled "Lines", attached to basket. Bag of Magic Beans - labelled "Magic Beans".

Scene Four

On Set
Back to the cottage scene.
1) Flash effect for Fairy reset.
2) Effect for Beanstalk set.
3) Fire blanket (offstage)

Personal Props
Alex: Bag of Magic Beans.
Jasmine: String of hankies etc.
Poppy: A3 cards
Old Woman: Wand (a bit bent, lights up) with "Lines" attached by peg.
Lawrence: Big bottle of pills.

Technical

For the cottage, we found that using 1½ inch wood was sufficiently strong, but light enough for the flats, coated in light muslin, which was painted. The back was solid, and the sides attached to the back using Velcro; the front was simply attached to the sides using hooks. These were easily released to allow the front to fall forwards, with the doorway falling over the Dame. We used a painted, light-weight bead curtain for the cottage door.

For the collapsing beanstalk, we used garden string for the stem with wire, in the shape of bean leaves, coated in green fabric for the body, with a box of extra bits for Act I, Scene One. The whole thing rigged to a piece of invisible fishing nylon over the back flats.

For the scary eyes in the woodland scene, we used glow sticks in painted toilet roll tubes, with eye shapes cut out - very effective.

For the Fairy's entrance, we hired a professional smoke machine, coupled with a very powerful photographer's flash unit. An alternative to smoke would be CO_2 for halls which do not allow smoke machines (it sets off the smoke alarms).

Sparking motor for final scene - we used fresh wire wool, wrapped around electrodes connected to a 12-volt battery, switched, inside a large clear container.